Emotional Manipulation

Gaslighting, Narcissistic Abuse

Cathleen R. Barton

I0625401

Emotional Manipulation: Gaslighting, Narcissistic Abuse

Table of Contents

Book 1 - Gaslighting

A Survivor's Guide to Healing and Empowerment After Psychological Abuse

01: What is Gaslighting?

Gaslighting is a form of psychological manipulation in which a person or group seeks to sow seeds of doubt in a targeted individual or group, making them question their own memory, perception, or judgment. It is a tactic often used by abusers, dictators, and cult leaders to control and subjugate their victims. The term "gaslighting" comes from the 1938 stage play "Gas Light," in which a husband tries to drive his wife crazy by dimming the gas lights in their home and then denying that the light changed when his wife points it out.

There are several tactics that are commonly used in gaslighting. One is denial, in which the manipulator flatly denies that something happened or that they said something, even when there is clear evidence to the contrary. This can leave the victim feeling confused and uncertain, and they may begin to question their own recollection of events.

Another tactic is lying and exaggerating, in which the manipulator makes false or exaggerated claims about the victim or about events that have occurred. This can cause the victim to doubt their own perception of reality and to feel that they are unreliable or untrustworthy.

Manipulators may also use the tactic of withholding information, in which they selectively provide or withhold information in order to confuse and mislead the victim. This can make it difficult for the victim to understand what is happening and can leave them feeling isolated and unsure of whom to trust.

A manipulator may also use the tactic of manipulating physical evidence, such as altering documents or hiding objects, in order to support their claims and create confusion. This can leave the victim feeling uncertain and unsure of what is true.

One of the most insidious tactics of gaslighting is projection, in which the manipulator accuses the victim of the very things that they themselves are guilty of. For example, an abuser may accuse their victim of being manipulative or abusive, even though it is the abuser who is behaving that way. This can leave the victim feeling confused and unsure of their own actions, and can be especially effective in causing the victim to doubt their own judgment.

The effects of gaslighting can be devastating, as it can leave the victim feeling confused, isolated, and unsure of their own perceptions and judgment. It can also cause the victim to become more dependent on the manipulator, as they may come to rely on them for a sense of stability and guidance. In extreme cases, gaslighting can lead to the victim developing mental health problems such as anxiety, depression, and PTSD.

It is important to recognize the signs of gaslighting and to seek help if you or someone you know is being victimized in this way. Some common signs include feeling confused or unsure of what is happening, feeling isolated or cut off from support, and feeling like you are going crazy. If you suspect that you or someone you know is being gaslighted, it is important to seek help from a trusted friend, family member, or mental health professional. It is also important to remember that you are not alone and that there is support available.

It is important to remember that gaslighting is a form of abuse, and it is never the fault of the victim. The manipulator is solely responsible for their actions, and it is important to hold them accountable for their behavior.

01: WHAT IS GASLIGHTING?

If you are being gaslighted, it is important to try to maintain a sense of reality and to seek out supportive relationships with friends and family members who can help you to stay grounded and to feel confident in your own perceptions and judgment. It can be helpful to keep a journal or a record of events, as this can help you to better understand what is happening and can serve as evidence if you need to seek help or report the abuse.

It is also important to remember that you have the right to set boundaries and to assert your own needs and wants. This may be difficult if you are being gaslighted, as the manipulator may try to control your behavior and limit your autonomy. However, it is important to stand up for yourself and to assert your own rights and needs. This may involve seeking help from a therapist or counselor, or it may involve seeking support from friends and family members.

If you are in an abusive relationship and are being gaslighted, it may be necessary to leave the relationship in order to protect yourself and your well-being. This can be a difficult and frightening decision, but it is important to remember that you deserve to be treated with respect and to be in a healthy, safe relationship. There are resources available to help you leave an abusive relationship, such as domestic violence shelters and hotlines, and it is important to reach out for help if you need it.

In conclusion, gaslighting is a harmful and abusive tactic that is used to manipulate and control others. It can have serious effects on the victim's mental health and well-being, and it is important to recognize the signs of gaslighting and to seek help if you or someone you know is being victimized in this way. Remember that you are not alone, and that there is support available to help you heal and to regain control over your life.

It is also important to remember that gaslighting is not just something that happens in personal relationships. It can also occur in professional settings, such as the workplace or in political contexts.

In the workplace, a manager or colleague may use gaslighting tactics to undermine an employee's confidence and to make them question their own abilities or judgment. This can be especially harmful if the employee is isolated or lacks support from their colleagues.

In political contexts, gaslighting can be used as a tactic to manipulate public opinion and to spread misinformation. This can be especially dangerous, as it can erode trust in institutions and undermine the foundations of democracy.

It is important to be aware of the potential for gaslighting in all types of relationships and to be alert to the signs of manipulation. It is also important to support and empower those who may be victims of gaslighting, and to hold manipulators accountable for their actions.

It is worth noting that it is possible for someone to gaslight themselves, particularly if they have low self-esteem or a history of being manipulated or abused. In these cases, it can be helpful to seek therapy or counseling to work through these issues and to build a stronger sense of self-worth and self-confidence.

Overall, gaslighting is a harmful and insidious form of manipulation that can have serious consequences for the victim. It is important to be aware of the signs of gaslighting and to seek help if you or someone you know is being victimized in this way. Remember that you deserve to be treated with respect and to be in healthy, supportive relationships, and that there is help available to support you in

01: WHAT IS GASLIGHTING?

achieving this.

02: The Signs of Gaslighting

Gaslighting is a form of psychological manipulation that can be difficult to recognize, especially if you are in a close relationship with the manipulator. However, there are several signs that can indicate that you or someone you know is being gaslighted.

One of the most common signs of gaslighting is feeling confused or unsure of what is happening. The manipulator may deny or distort events, or may withhold information, in order to create confusion and uncertainty. As a result, the victim may feel like they are "going crazy" or like they can't trust their own perceptions.

Another sign of gaslighting is feeling isolated or cut off from support. The manipulator may try to isolate the victim from friends and family, or may try to undermine their relationships with others, in order to make them more reliant on the manipulator. This can leave the victim feeling alone and unsure of whom to trust.

A third sign of gaslighting is feeling like you are constantly second-guessing yourself or doubting your own judgment. The manipulator may try to undermine the victim's confidence in their own abilities or judgment, and may try to make them feel incompetent or incapable. This can leave the victim feeling insecure and unsure of themselves.

A fourth sign of gaslighting is experiencing a change in your personality or behavior. The manipulator may try to control the victim's behavior or to make them conform to their expectations, and this can lead to the victim changing their personality or behavior in order to please the manipulator.

A fifth sign of gaslighting is experiencing a change in your relationships with others. The manipulator may try to alienate the victim from their friends and family, or may try to manipulate the victim's relationships with others in order to further their own goals. This can leave the victim feeling isolated and alone.

It is worth noting that not all of these signs necessarily indicate that someone is being gaslighted. However, if you are experiencing several of these signs, or if you are feeling confused, uncertain, or isolated, it may be worth considering the possibility that you are being manipulated.

It is important to remember that if you are being gaslighted, it is not your fault. The manipulator is solely responsible for their behavior, and it is important to hold them accountable for their actions. If you are in an abusive relationship and are being gaslighted, it may be necessary to leave the relationship in order to protect yourself and your well-being.

There are resources available to help you leave an abusive relationship, such as domestic violence shelters and hotlines, and it is important to reach out for help if you need it.

If you suspect that you or someone you know is being gaslighted, it is important to seek help from a trusted friend, family member, or mental health professional. It is also important to remember that you are not alone and that there is support available to help you heal and to regain control over your life.

It can be especially difficult to recognize the signs of gaslighting if you are in a close relationship with the manipulator, as they may have gained your trust and may have convinced you that they have your best interests at heart. However, it is important to be aware of the potential for manipulation and to be alert to the signs that something may be wrong.

Some other signs of gaslighting to watch out for include:

02: THE SIGNS OF GASLIGHTING

– The manipulator consistently contradicts your perceptions or memories of events, even when you are sure you are right.

– The manipulator frequently changes the subject or distracts you when you try to discuss something that is important to you.

– The manipulator minimizes your feelings or concerns, or makes you feel like you are being oversensitive or unreasonable.

– The manipulator tries to make you feel guilty or ashamed for things that are not your fault.

– The manipulator tries to control your behavior or decisions, or makes you feel like you have to ask permission for things.

– The manipulator tries to turn others against you, or undermines your relationships with friends and family.

If you are experiencing these signs, it is important to take them seriously and to seek help if you need it. Remember that you have the right to be treated with respect and to be in healthy, supportive relationships, and that you deserve to feel safe and valued.

It is also important to be aware of the potential for gaslighting in professional or political contexts. In these settings, manipulators may use similar tactics to undermine your confidence, to spread misinformation, or to control public opinion. It is important to be aware of these tactics and to be vigilant against them.

Overall, the signs of gaslighting can be subtle and may not be immediately obvious. However, if you are experiencing confusion, uncertainty, or a sense that something is not right, it is important to trust your instincts and to seek help if you need it. Remember that you are not alone and that there is support available to help you heal and to regain control over your life.

It is also important to recognize that gaslighting is a form of abuse, and it is never the victim's fault. The manipulator is solely responsible for their actions, and it is important to hold them accountable for their behavior.

If you are in a relationship with someone who is gaslighting you, it can be difficult to know what to do. It is important to remember that you have the right to set boundaries and to assert your own needs and wants. This may involve setting limits on the time you spend with the manipulator or on the types of conversations you have with them. It may also involve seeking support from friends and family or from a therapist or counselor.

If you are in an abusive relationship and are being gaslighted, it may be necessary to leave the relationship in order to protect yourself and your well-being. This can be a difficult and frightening decision, but it is important to remember that you deserve to be treated with respect and to be in a healthy, safe relationship. There are resources available to help you leave an abusive relationship, such as domestic violence shelters and hotlines, and it is important to reach out for help if you need it.

It is also important to remember that it is possible to recover from gaslighting and to rebuild your sense of self-worth and self-confidence. This may involve seeking therapy or counseling, or it may involve building new, supportive relationships with friends and family. It is important to be patient with yourself and to give yourself time to heal.

In conclusion, gaslighting is a harmful and abusive tactic that can have serious consequences for the victim. It is important to recognize the signs of gaslighting and to seek help if you or someone you know is being victimized in this way. Remember that you are not alone, and that there is support available to help you heal and to regain control over your life.

03: The Impact of Gaslighting on Your Mental Health

Gaslighting is a form of psychological manipulation in which a person or group seeks to sow seeds of doubt in a targeted individual, making them question their own memory, perception, or judgment. Gaslighting can occur in personal relationships, at work, or in political or social groups. It is often a subtle form of abuse, as the manipulator may try to convince their victim that they are simply misunderstanding things or are overly sensitive. However, the effects of gaslighting can be severe and long-lasting, causing serious damage to a person's mental health and well-being.

One of the most insidious aspects of gaslighting is that it can be difficult to detect, especially if the manipulator is skilled at concealing their true intentions. They may deny saying or doing certain things, or present conflicting information in a way that leaves the victim feeling confused and uncertain. This can lead to the victim feeling isolated and disconnected from their own reality, as they struggle to make sense of what is happening around them.

The constant questioning of one's own perceptions and

memories can be emotionally and mentally exhausting, leading to feelings of anxiety, depression, and low self-esteem. The victim may also feel a sense of powerlessness and helplessness, as they are unable to control the manipulation or stop it from happening. In some cases, they may begin to doubt their own sanity, leading to serious mental health issues such as paranoia, dissociation, and even psychosis.

Gaslighting can also have a profound impact on a person's relationships and social interactions. The manipulator may try to alienate the victim from their friends and family, further isolating them and making it more difficult for them to seek support. The victim may also become more reliant on the manipulator for emotional support, leading to an unhealthy dynamic in which they are constantly seeking validation and approval from their abuser.

There are several ways in which a person can protect themselves from the effects of gaslighting. It is important to be aware of the signs of gaslighting and to trust one's own perceptions and instincts. It can also be helpful to seek support from trusted friends, family members, or a mental health professional. It is also important to set boundaries and to communicate openly and honestly with the manipulator, letting them know that their behavior is not acceptable.

In some cases, it may be necessary to seek help from a legal or social services agency in order to protect oneself from on-going abuse. It is also important to remember that no one deserves to be subjected to gaslighting or any other form of psychological abuse, and that it is never too late to seek help and make positive changes in one's life.

In conclusion, gaslighting is a serious form of psychological manipulation that can have a devastating impact on a person's mental health and well-being. It is important to be aware of the signs of gaslighting and to seek support in order to protect oneself from its harmful effects. With the right help and support, it is possible to break free from the cycle of abuse and to reclaim one's own sense of self and reality.

It is important to recognize that gaslighting is a form of abuse and that it can have serious consequences for a person's mental health. If you suspect that you or someone you know is being gaslighted, it is important to seek help and support.

03: THE IMPACT OF GASLIGHTING ON YOUR MENTAL HEALTH

There are several resources available for individuals who are experiencing gaslighting or other forms of abuse. These may include therapy or counseling, support groups, or legal or social services agencies. These resources can provide the necessary support and guidance to help individuals cope with the effects of gaslighting and to develop healthy coping strategies.

It is also important to remember that it is never too late to seek help and to make positive changes in one's life. No one deserves to be subjected to gaslighting or any other form of abuse, and it is possible to break free from the cycle of abuse and to reclaim one's own sense of self and reality.

It is important to recognize that gaslighting can have serious and long-lasting effects on a person's mental health and well-being. If you or someone you know is experiencing gaslighting or other forms of abuse, it is important to seek help and support as soon as possible. With the right resources and support, it is possible to break free from the cycle of abuse and to rebuild one's sense of self and reality.

It is important to recognize that gaslighting can be a subtle and insidious form of abuse, and that it can be difficult for a victim to identify and acknowledge what is happening to them. This can make it difficult for them to seek help and support, as they may not realize the full extent of the manipulation and abuse they are experiencing.

One of the most important things a victim of gaslighting can do is to seek support from trusted friends, family members, or a mental health professional. These individuals can provide a sense of grounding and help the victim to validate their own perceptions and experiences. It can also be helpful to seek out a support group or therapy, where the victim can connect with others who have experienced similar abuse and can learn healthy coping strategies.

It is also important for victims of gaslighting to set boundaries and to communicate openly and honestly with the manipulator. This can help to establish clear expectations and to assert control over the situation. In some cases, it may be necessary to seek help from a legal or social services agency in order to protect oneself from ongoing abuse.

It is also important to remember that it is never too late to seek help and to make positive changes in one's life. No one deserves to be subjected to gaslighting or any other form of abuse, and it is possible to break free from the cycle of abuse and to reclaim one's own sense of self and reality.

In conclusion, the impact of gaslighting on mental health can be severe and long-lasting. It is important to recognize the signs of gaslighting and to seek help and support in order to protect oneself from its harmful effects. With the right resources and support, it is possible to break free from the cycle of abuse and to rebuild one's sense of self and reality.

04: The Cycle of Gaslighting and How to Break Free

The cycle of gaslighting is a pattern of manipulation and abuse that can be difficult for a victim to recognize and break free from. Gaslighting is a form of psychological manipulation in which a person or group seeks to sow seeds of doubt in a targeted individual, making them question their own memory, perception, or judgment. Gaslighting can occur in personal relationships, at work, or in political or social groups. It is often a subtle form of abuse, as the manipulator may try to convince their victim that they are simply misunderstanding things or are overly sensitive.

The cycle of gaslighting typically begins with the manipulator planting seeds of doubt in the victim's mind. This may involve denying saying or doing certain things, or presenting conflicting information in a way that leaves the victim feeling confused and uncertain. The manipulator may also try to alienate the victim from their friends and family, making it more difficult for them to seek support or validation from others.

As the cycle continues, the victim may begin to doubt their own perceptions and memories, leading to feelings of anxiety, depression, and low self-esteem. They may also feel a sense of powerlessness and helplessness, as they are unable to control the manipulation or stop it from happening. In some cases, they may even begin to doubt their own sanity, leading to serious mental health issues such as paranoia, dissociation, and psychosis.

The cycle of gaslighting can be difficult to break, as the manipulator may be skilled at concealing their true intentions and at making the victim feel like they are the problem. However, there are steps that a victim of gaslighting can take to break free from this cycle and to reclaim their sense of self and reality.

One of the most important things a victim of gaslighting can do is to seek support from trusted friends, family members, or a mental health professional. These individuals can provide a sense of grounding and help the victim to validate their own perceptions and experiences. It can also be helpful to seek out a support group or therapy, where the victim can connect with others who have experienced similar abuse and can learn healthy coping strategies.

It is also important for victims of gaslighting to set boundaries and to communicate openly and honestly with the manipulator. This can help to establish clear expectations and to assert control over the situation. In some cases, it may be necessary to seek help from a legal or social services agency in order to protect oneself from ongoing abuse.

It is also important for victims of gaslighting to practice self-care and to engage in activities that promote their own well-being. This may include exercising, engaging in hobbies, or seeking out activities that bring them joy and fulfillment. Taking care of oneself can help to build resilience and to provide a sense of stability and purpose, which can be especially important during times of uncertainty and stress.

Breaking free from the cycle of gaslighting can be a challenging and difficult process, but it is possible with the right support and resources. It is important to remember that no one deserves to be subjected to gaslighting or any other form of abuse, and that it is never too late to seek help and make positive changes in one's life. By seeking support and learning healthy coping strategies, victims of gaslighting can break free from the cycle of abuse and reclaim their sense of self and reality.

It is also important for victims of gaslighting to be aware of the signs of gaslighting and to trust their own perceptions and instincts. This can help them to recognize when they are being manipulated and to seek help and support before the cycle of abuse becomes more entrenched. Some common signs of gaslighting may include:

– Denial of events or actions: The manipulator may deny saying or doing certain things, even when confronted with evidence to the contrary.

– Presenting conflicting information: The manipulator may present conflicting information in a way that leaves the victim feeling confused and uncertain.

– Isolating the victim: The manipulator may try to alienate the victim from their friends and family, making it more difficult for them to seek support or validation from others.

– Diminishing the victim's accomplishments: The manipulator may attempt to belittle or diminish the victim's accomplishments in order to make them feel incompetent or unworthy.

04: THE CYCLE OF GASLIGHTING AND HOW TO BREAK FREE

– Blaming the victim: The manipulator may attempt to shift blame onto the victim, making them feel responsible for the manipulator's behavior.

It is important for victims of gaslighting to be aware of these signs and to trust their own perceptions and instincts. If you suspect that you or someone you know is being gaslighted, it is important to seek help and support as soon as possible. With the right resources and support, it is possible to break free from the cycle of abuse and to reclaim your sense of self and reality.

In conclusion, the cycle of gaslighting is a pattern of manipulation and abuse that can have serious and long-lasting effects on a person's mental health and well-being. It is important to be aware of the signs of gaslighting and to seek help and support in order to break free from this cycle. With the right resources and support, it is possible to break free from the cycle of abuse and to reclaim your sense of self and reality. So, it is very important to recognize the signs of gaslighting and take necessary actions to break free from it.

It is also important for individuals who have experienced gaslighting to be mindful of their own mental health and to

seek help if needed. The effects of gaslighting can be severe
and long-lasting, and it is important to address any mental
health issues that may arise as a result of the abuse. This
may include seeking therapy or counseling, joining a support group, or seeking help from a mental health professional.

It is also important for individuals who have experienced
gaslighting to practice self-care and to engage in activities
that promote their own well-being. This may include exercising, engaging in hobbies, or seeking out activities that
bring them joy and fulfillment. Taking care of oneself can
help to build resilience and to provide a sense of stability
and purpose, which can be especially important during
times of uncertainty and stress.

It is also important for individuals who have experienced
gaslighting to be mindful of their relationships and to surround themselves with supportive and caring individuals.
This may involve seeking out new friendships or building
healthier relationships with existing friends and family
members. It may also be necessary to set boundaries with
individuals who are not supportive or who engage in manip-

ulative or abusive behaviors.

Breaking free from the cycle of gaslighting can be a difficult and challenging process, but it is possible with the right support and resources. It is important to remember that no one deserves to be subjected to gaslighting or any other form of abuse, and that it is never too late to seek help and make positive changes in one's life. By seeking support and learning healthy coping strategies, individuals who have experienced gaslighting can break free from the cycle of abuse and reclaim their sense of self and reality.

05: The Role of Boundaries in Healing from Gaslighting

Boundaries are an important aspect of healthy relationships and can play a crucial role in the healing process for individuals who have experienced gaslighting or other forms of abuse. Gaslighting is a form of psychological manipulation in which a person or group seeks to sow seeds of doubt in a targeted individual, making them question their own memory, perception, or judgment. Gaslighting can occur in personal relationships, at work, or in political or social groups. It is often a subtle form of abuse, as the manipulator may try to convince their victim that they are simply misunderstanding things or are overly sensitive.

One of the most harmful effects of gaslighting is that it can leave victims feeling isolated and disconnected from their own reality. They may feel confused and uncertain about what is happening around them, and may struggle to trust their own perceptions and instincts. Setting boundaries is an important part of the healing process, as it helps individuals to reclaim their own sense of self and to assert control over their lives.

There are several types of boundaries that can be helpful for individuals who are healing from gaslighting. Physical boundaries involve setting limits on physical touch and proximity, and may include things like respecting personal space or setting rules about when and how physical contact is acceptable. Emotional boundaries involve setting limits on how much of one's own emotions and personal information are shared with others, and may include things like setting limits on how much emotional support is given or received. Mental boundaries involve setting limits on what information and ideas one is willing to accept or consider, and may include things like setting limits on how much time is spent engaging in certain activities or with certain people.

Setting boundaries can be a challenging process, especially for individuals who have experienced gaslighting or other forms of abuse. It may be difficult to assert control over one's own life and to set limits with manipulators or abusers. However, it is important to remember that setting boundaries is an important part of the healing process, and that it is possible to learn healthy ways of interacting with others.

There are several ways in which individuals can set and enforce boundaries in their relationships. One of the most effective ways is to communicate openly and honestly with others about what is and is not acceptable. This may involve setting clear limits and expectations, and being firm and assertive when these limits are crossed. It is also important to be consistent in enforcing boundaries, and to follow through with any consequences that may be necessary if boundaries are not respected.

Another important aspect of setting boundaries is learning to say "no" when necessary. This may involve setting limits on how much time or energy is given to others, or saying "no" to requests or demands that are not in one's own best interests. It is important to remember that it is okay to prioritize one's own needs and to set limits on how much time and energy is given to others.

It is also important for individuals who are healing from gaslighting to seek support from trusted friends, family members, or a mental health professional. These individuals can provide a sense of grounding and can help individuals to validate their own perceptions and experiences. It can also be helpful to seek out a support group or therapy, where individuals can connect with others who have experienced similar abuse and can learn healthy coping strategies.

In conclusion, boundaries play an important role in the healing process for individuals who have experienced gaslighting or other forms of abuse. Setting and enforcing boundaries can help individuals to reclaim their own sense of self and to assert control over their lives. It is important to communicate openly and honestly with others, to be consistent in enforcing boundaries, and to seek support from trusted individuals in order to learn healthy ways of interacting with others.

It is important for individuals who are healing from gaslighting to be mindful of their own mental health and to seek help if needed. The effects of gaslighting can be severe and long-lasting, and it is important to address any mental health issues that may arise as a result of the abuse. This may include seeking therapy or counseling, joining a support group, or seeking help from a mental health professional.

It is also important for individuals who are healing from gaslighting to practice self-care and to engage in activities that promote their own well-being. This may include exercising, engaging in hobbies, or seeking out activities that bring them joy and fulfillment. Taking care of oneself can help to build resilience and to provide a sense of stability and purpose, which can be especially important during times of uncertainty and stress.

It is also important for individuals who are healing from gaslighting to be mindful of their relationships and to surround themselves with supportive and caring individuals. This may involve seeking out new friendships or building healthier relationships with existing friends and family members. It may also be necessary to set boundaries with individuals who are not supportive or who engage in manipulative or abusive behaviors.

Healing from gaslighting can be a challenging and difficult process, but it is possible with the right support and resources. It is important to remember that no one deserves to be subjected to gaslighting or any other form of abuse, and that it is never too late to seek help and make positive changes in one's life. By seeking support and learning healthy coping strategies, individuals who have experienced gaslighting can break free from the cycle of abuse and reclaim their sense of self and reality.

It is also important for individuals who are healing from gaslighting to be aware of the potential triggers that may cause them to feel vulnerable or uncertain. Triggers may include certain people, places, or situations that remind the individual of the abuse they experienced. By being aware of these triggers, individuals can take steps to protect themselves and to maintain their own sense of stability and well-being.

One way to cope with triggers is to develop a plan for how to respond when they occur. This may involve seeking support from trusted friends or family members, practicing self-care activities, or seeking out a safe and supportive environment. It may also be helpful to talk through the trigger with a therapist or counselor, in order to better understand and manage the feelings that are associated with it.

It is also important for individuals who are healing from gaslighting to work on rebuilding their sense of self and trust in their own perceptions and instincts. This may involve seeking therapy or counseling, joining a support

group, or engaging in activities that promote self-awareness
and self-esteem. It is also important to remember that healing is a process and that it is okay to take things one step at
a time.

In conclusion, healing from gaslighting is a process that requires time, patience, and support. By setting boundaries,
seeking support, practicing self-care, and being aware of
triggers, individuals who have experienced gaslighting can
work towards rebuilding their sense of self and trust in their
own perceptions and instincts. It is important to remember
that no one deserves to be subjected to gaslighting or any
other form of abuse, and that it is never too late to seek help
and make positive changes in one's life.

06: The Importance of a Support System

Having a support system is an important aspect of mental health and well-being, and can be especially crucial for individuals who have experienced trauma or abuse. A support system can provide a sense of connection and belonging, and can offer emotional, practical, and social support. It can help individuals to feel less isolated and alone, and can provide a sense of hope and resilience during difficult times.

There are many different types of support systems, and what works best for one person may not be the same for another. Some people may find support through friends and family, while others may find it through professional support networks such as therapy or counseling. It is important for individuals to identify what types of support work best for them, and to build a support system that meets their needs.

One of the most important aspects of a support system is the ability to provide emotional support. This may involve listening to and validating an individual's experiences, offering words of encouragement or comfort, or simply being present for them during difficult times. Emotional support can help individuals to feel less alone and to cope with difficult emotions, and can be an important factor in helping them to heal and move forward.

Practical support can also be an important aspect of a support system. This may involve providing assistance with tasks such as grocery shopping or running errands, or offering financial or other resources. Practical support can help individuals to feel more secure and less overwhelmed, and can make a significant difference in their daily lives.

Social support is another important aspect of a support system. This may involve engaging in activities or hobbies with friends or family, or simply spending time together in a supportive and caring environment. Social support can help individuals to feel less isolated and more connected to others, and can provide a sense of meaning and purpose.

Having a support system is not always easy, and it may take time and effort to build a network of supportive relationships.

There are several steps that individuals can take to build a support system:

06: THE IMPORTANCE OF A SUPPORT SYSTEM

– Identify what types of support are most important to you: This may include emotional, practical, or social support, or a combination of all three. It is important to be honest with yourself about what you need and to seek out support that meets those needs.

– Reach out to others: It can be intimidating to ask for help, but it is important to remember that most people are willing to offer support if asked. Reach out to friends, family, or professionals and let them know what you need. It may also be helpful to join a support group or to seek out other resources such as therapy or counseling.

– Be open and honest: In order to receive support, it is important to be open and honest about your needs and feelings. This may involve sharing your experiences, talking about your emotions, or simply expressing a need for support. By being open and honest, you can build deeper and more meaningful relationships with others.

– Be willing to accept and give support: Support is a two-way street, and it is important to be willing to both give and receive support. This may involve offering practical or emotional support to others, or simply being present and available when needed. It is also important to be willing to accept support when it is offered, and to be open to trying new things or seeking help when needed.

– Take care of yourself: Building a support system is an important aspect of self-care, but it is not the only aspect. It is important to engage in activities that promote your own well-being, such as exercising, eating a healthy diet, and getting enough sleep. By taking care of yourself, you can build resilience and be better equipped to handle challenges and setbacks.

In conclusion, having a support system is an important aspect of mental health and well-being. It can provide a sense of connection and belonging, and can offer emotional, practical, and social support. There are many different types of support systems, and it is important for individuals to identify what works best for them and to build a support system that meets their needs. By reaching out to others, being open and honest, being willing to give and receive support, and taking care of themselves, individuals can build a strong and supportive network of relationships.

It is important to remember that building a support system

is a process, and that it may take time and effort to develop meaningful relationships. It is also important to be patient with yourself and to recognize that it is okay to take things one step at a time. Building a support system is not always easy, and it may involve facing challenges or setbacks along the way. However, with patience and persistence, it is possible to build a strong and supportive network of relationships that can provide a sense of connection, belonging, and hope during difficult times.

It is also important to be mindful of your own needs and boundaries when building a support system. It is okay to set limits on what you are willing and able to give, and to prioritize your own well-being. It is also important to be aware of any patterns of unhealthy or manipulative behavior in your relationships, and to set boundaries with individuals who are not supportive or who engage in abusive or manipulative behaviors.

Finally, it is important to remember that it is okay to seek help if you are struggling to build a support system or to cope with difficult emotions or experiences. Seeking help from a mental health professional or joining a support group can be an important step in the healing process, and can provide valuable resources and support.

In conclusion, the importance of a support system cannot be overstated. It can provide a sense of connection and belonging, and can offer emotional, practical, and social support. Building a support system is a process that may take time and effort, but with patience and persistence, it is possible to develop meaningful and supportive relationships. It is also important to be mindful of your own needs and boundaries, and to seek help if needed. By building a strong and supportive network of relationships, individuals can find hope and resilience during difficult times.

07: The Role of Counseling in Healing from Psychological Abuse

Counseling can be an important tool for individuals who are seeking to heal from psychological abuse. Psychological abuse, also known as emotional abuse or mental abuse, is a pattern of behavior that seeks to undermine an individual's sense of self-worth and confidence. It can involve things like manipulation, coercion, blame, criticism, or isolation, and can have serious and long-lasting effects on an individual's mental health and well-being.

Counseling can provide a safe and supportive environment for individuals to explore their experiences and emotions, and to work through the impact of abuse on their lives. It can also provide a space for individuals to learn healthy coping strategies and to develop a stronger sense of self and self-worth.

There are several ways in which counseling can be helpful for individuals who are healing from psychological abuse:

– Providing a safe and supportive environment: Counseling provides a space where individuals can feel safe and supported as they explore their experiences and emotions. This can be especially important for individuals who have experienced abuse, as it can help to build a sense of trust and openness that is necessary for healing.

– Validating experiences and emotions: Counseling can provide a space for individuals to have their experiences and emotions validated. This can be especially important for individuals who have experienced abuse, as they may feel that their feelings and perspectives are not being respected or understood. Validating an individual's experiences and emotions can help to build a sense of trust and can be an important step in the healing process.

– Exploring coping strategies: Counseling can provide a space for individuals to explore different coping strategies and to find what works best for them. This may involve learning new skills such as stress management or communication, or finding healthy ways to manage difficult emotions. Counseling can help individuals to develop a toolkit of coping strategies that they can draw upon in times of stress or hardship.

– Building self-worth and confidence: Counseling can help individuals to rebuild their sense of self-worth and confid-

ence, which can be particularly important for those who
have experienced abuse. Counseling can provide a space for
individuals to work through any negative beliefs or self-
doubt that may have been instilled by the abuser, and to develop a stronger sense of self and self-worth.

– Providing support and guidance: Counseling can provide
ongoing support and guidance as individuals navigate the
healing process. This can be especially helpful for individuals who are struggling to cope with the aftermath of abuse,
and may feel overwhelmed or uncertain about what to do
next. Counseling can provide a sense of direction and can
help individuals to feel less alone and isolated as they work
towards healing and recovery.

There are several different types of counseling that may be
helpful for individuals who are healing from psychological
abuse. Some common approaches include cognitive-behavioral therapy (CBT), dialectical behavior therapy (DBT), and
trauma-focused therapy. These approaches may involve
learning new coping strategies, exploring one's thoughts
and feelings, or working through traumatic experiences in a
safe and supportive environment. It is important for indi-

viduals to find a therapist who is trained in working with individuals who have experienced abuse, and who is able to provide the support and guidance that is needed.

It is important to remember that healing from psychological abuse is a process, and that it may take time and effort. Counseling can be an important tool in this process, and can provide a safe and supportive environment for individuals to explore their experiences and emotions, and to develop healthy coping strategies. By seeking counseling and support, individuals can work towards healing and recovery, and can build a stronger sense of self and self-worth.

It is also important for individuals who are seeking counseling to be patient with themselves and to recognize that healing is a process that may involve setbacks and challenges. It is important to be kind to oneself and to take things one step at a time. It is also important to be open to trying new things and to seeking additional support if needed.

It is also important for individuals who are seeking counseling to be aware of their own needs and boundaries, and to communicate these to their therapist. This may involve setting limits on the types of topics that are discussed, or setting boundaries around the amount of time and energy that is given to the therapy process. It is important to remember that it is okay to prioritize one's own well-being and to set limits when needed.

In conclusion, counseling can be an important tool for individuals who are seeking to heal from psychological abuse. It can provide a safe and supportive environment for individuals to explore their experiences and emotions, and to develop healthy coping strategies. By seeking counseling and support, individuals can work towards healing and recovery, and can build a stronger sense of self and self-worth. It is important to be patient with oneself, to be open to trying new things, and to be aware of one's own needs and boundaries in the therapy process.

08: The Process of Empowerment After Gaslighting

Empowerment is the process of regaining control over one's own life and well-being, and can be an important step in the healing process after experiencing gaslighting. Gaslighting is a form of psychological abuse that involves manipulating an individual's sense of reality, often in order to exert control over them. It can involve things like denying events or experiences, manipulating information, or causing the individual to doubt their own perceptions and memories. Gaslighting can have serious and long-lasting effects on an individual's mental health and well-being, and can make it difficult for them to trust their own thoughts and feelings.

The process of empowerment after gaslighting involves reclaiming one's own sense of self and reality, and rebuilding a sense of trust in oneself and one's own perceptions. It may involve seeking out support and resources, setting boundaries, and developing healthy coping strategies. Empowerment is a process that may take time and effort, but with patience and persistence, it is possible to regain control over one's own life and to move forward in a positive direction.

There are several steps that individuals can take to begin

08: THE PROCESS OF EMPOWERMENT AFTER GAS- LIGHTING

the process of empowerment after experiencing gaslighting:

– Seek out support and resources: It is important for individuals who are healing from gaslighting to seek out support and resources that can help them to rebuild their sense of self and trust in their own perceptions. This may involve seeking therapy or counseling, joining a support group, or seeking help from a trusted friend or family member.

– Set boundaries: Setting boundaries is an important aspect of empowerment after experiencing gaslighting. This may involve setting limits on the types of interactions or behaviors that are acceptable, or setting limits on the amount of time and energy that is given to certain relationships or activities. Setting boundaries can help individuals to protect their own well-being and to feel more in control of their own lives.

– Develop healthy coping strategies: Developing healthy coping strategies can be an important step in the process of empowerment after gaslighting. This may involve learning new skills such as stress management or communication, or finding healthy ways to manage difficult emotions. It may also involve finding activities or hobbies that bring joy and fulfillment, and that help to build a sense of purpose and meaning.

– Rebuild trust in oneself: Rebuilding trust in oneself can be a challenging but important aspect of the empowerment process after experiencing gaslighting. This may involve challenging negative beliefs or self-doubt that may have been instilled by the abuser, and rebuilding a sense of self-worth and confidence. It may also involve finding ways to validate one's own experiences and emotions, and to trust in one's own perceptions and instincts.

Empowerment after gaslighting is a process that may involve challenges and setbacks, but with patience and persistence, it is possible to reclaim control over one's own life and to move forward in a positive direction. It is important to be kind to oneself and to recognize that healing is a process that may take time. By seeking out support and resources, setting boundaries, developing healthy coping strategies, and rebuilding trust in oneself, individuals can work towards empowerment and recovery after experiencing gaslighting.

It is also important for individuals who are working towards empowerment after gaslighting to be mindful of their own needs and boundaries, and to prioritize their own well-being. This may involve taking breaks or setting limits on certain activities or relationships, or seeking additional support if needed. It is important to remember that it is okay to put one's own needs first and to prioritize self-care.

It is also important to be aware of any potential triggers that may arise during the empowerment process. Triggers are things that may remind an individual of the abuse they experienced, and can cause them to feel vulnerable or uncertain. By being aware of these triggers, individuals can take steps to protect themselves and to maintain their own sense of stability and well-being.

In conclusion, the process of empowerment after gaslighting involves reclaiming control over one's own life and well-being, and rebuilding a sense of trust in oneself and one's own perceptions. It may involve seeking out support and resources, setting boundaries, and developing healthy coping strategies. Empowerment is a process that may take time and effort, but with patience and persistence, it is possible to move forward in a positive direction. It is important to be mindful of one's own needs and boundaries, and to be aware of any potential triggers that may arise during the empowerment process. By taking these steps, individuals can work towards empowerment and recovery after experiencing gaslighting.

It is important to remember that the process of empowerment after gaslighting is unique to each individual, and what works for one person may not be the same for another. It is important for individuals to be patient with themselves and to recognize that healing is a process that may involve setbacks and challenges. It is also important to be open to trying new things and to seeking additional support if needed.

It is also important to be aware of any patterns of unhealthy or abusive behavior in one's relationships, and to set boundaries with individuals who are not supportive or who engage in abusive or manipulative behaviors. This may involve seeking therapy or counseling, or seeking help from a trusted friend or family member. By setting boundaries and seeking support, individuals can work towards building healthy and supportive relationships that are based on respect and trust.

It is also important for individuals who are working towards empowerment after gaslighting to be mindful of their own self-care and well-being. This may involve engaging in activities that promote physical and emotional health, such as exercising, eating a healthy diet, and getting enough sleep. By taking care of oneself, individuals can build resilience and be better equipped to handle challenges and setbacks.

In conclusion, the process of empowerment after gaslighting is a unique and individualized process that involves reclaiming control over one's own life and well-being, and rebuilding a sense of trust in oneself and one's own perceptions. It may involve seeking out support and resources, setting boundaries, and developing healthy coping strategies. By being patient with oneself, open to trying new things, and mindful of one's own self-care and well-being, individuals can work towards empowerment and recovery after experiencing gaslighting.

09: Rediscovering Your Worth and Building Self-Esteem

Rediscovering one's worth and building self-esteem are important steps in the process of personal growth and development. Self-esteem is defined as an individual's overall sense of self-worth and confidence, and is an important aspect of mental health and well-being. When we have healthy self-esteem, we are more likely to feel confident and capable, and to take risks and pursue our goals. When our self-esteem is low, we may feel uncertain or unworthy, and may struggle to take care of ourselves or to set healthy boundaries.

Rediscovering one's worth and building self-esteem can be a challenging but rewarding process, and may involve exploring one's own values, setting goals, and learning new skills. It is important to be patient with oneself and to recognize that building self-esteem is a process that may take time and effort.

There are several steps that individuals can take to rediscover their worth and build self-esteem:

– Explore your values: One of the first steps in rediscovering your worth and building self-esteem is to explore your own values and beliefs. This may involve asking yourself questions such as "What is important to me?", "What are my goals and aspirations?", and "What makes me feel fulfilled and satisfied?" By exploring your own values, you can begin to understand what is most important to you and to build a sense of purpose and direction in your life.

– Set goals: Setting goals is an important aspect of building self-esteem, as it provides a sense of direction and helps to focus our energy and efforts. Goals can be short-term or long-term, and can be related to various areas of our lives such as career, relationships, personal growth, or health and wellness. By setting goals and working towards their achievement, we can build a sense of accomplishment and self-worth.

– Learn new skills: Learning new skills is a great way to build self-esteem and to feel more confident and capable. This may involve learning a new hobby or skill, or pursuing education or training in a particular area. By challenging ourselves and expanding our knowledge and abilities, we can build self-esteem and feel more confident in our own abilities.

– Practice self-care: Taking care of ourselves is an important aspect of building self-esteem, as it helps us to feel more capable and in control of our lives. Self-care can involve things like exercising, eating a healthy diet, getting enough sleep, and taking time for relaxation and leisure. By taking care of ourselves, we can build resilience and feel more capable of handling challenges and setbacks.

– Seek support and resources: Seeking support and resources can be an important aspect of building self-esteem, especially if we are struggling with low self-esteem or self-doubt. This may involve seeking therapy or counseling, joining a support group, or seeking help from a trusted friend or family member. By seeking support and resources, we can gain valuable perspective and guidance, and can build a stronger sense of self-worth and confidence.

– Set boundaries: Setting boundaries is an important aspect of building self-esteem, as it helps us to protect our own well-being and to feel more in control of our lives. Boundaries can be physical, emotional, or mental, and may involve setting limits on the types of interactions or behaviors that are acceptable, or setting limits on the amount of time and energy that is given to certain relationships or activities. By setting boundaries, we can feel more in control of our own lives and more able to take care of ourselves.

– Practice gratitude: Practicing gratitude is a simple but powerful way to build self-esteem and to feel more positive and hopeful. This may involve keeping a gratitude journal or making a list of things that we are thankful for each day. By focusing on the things that are going well in our lives, we can build a sense of appreciation and positivity, and can feel more confident and capable.

– Seek positive role models: Seeking positive role models can be a helpful way to build self-esteem and to gain perspective on what is possible. This may involve finding individuals who inspire us or who have achieved success in areas that are important to us. By seeking positive role models, we can gain insight and inspiration, and can feel more motivated and capable of achieving our own goals.

In conclusion, rediscovering one's worth and building self-esteem are important steps in the process of personal growth and development. It is a process that may take time and effort, and may involve exploring one's values, setting goals, learning new skills, practicing self-care, seeking support and resources, setting boundaries, practicing gratitude, and seeking positive role models. By taking these steps, individuals can build a stronger sense of self-worth and confidence, and can feel more capable and in control of their own lives.

It is important to remember that building self-esteem is a process that may involve challenges and setbacks, and it is important to be patient with oneself and to recognize that it is a journey. It is also important to be kind to oneself and to recognize that we are all human and that it is okay to make mistakes. By practicing self-compassion and by focusing on our strengths and accomplishments, we can build self-esteem and feel more positive and confident.

It is also important to be aware of negative self-talk and to challenge negative beliefs or thoughts that may be hindering our self-esteem. Negative self-talk can be damaging to our self-esteem and can hold us back from achieving our goals. By recognizing and challenging negative self-talk, we can build a stronger sense of self-worth and confidence.

09: REDISCOVERING YOUR WORTH AND BUILDING SELF-ESTEEM

It is also important to be open to seeking support and resources if needed. This may involve seeking therapy or counseling, joining a support group, or seeking help from a trusted friend or family member. By seeking support, we can gain valuable perspective and guidance, and can build a stronger sense of self-worth and confidence.

In conclusion, building self-esteem is a process that involves exploring one's values, setting goals, learning new skills, practicing self-care, seeking support and resources, setting boundaries, practicing gratitude, and seeking positive role models. It is a process that may involve challenges and setbacks, and it is important to be patient with oneself and to recognize that it is a journey. By being kind to oneself, recognizing and challenging negative self-talk, and seeking support and resources if needed, individuals can build self-esteem and feel more positive and confident.

10: The Role of Self-Care in the Healing Process

Self-care is an important aspect of the healing process, and involves taking care of one's own physical, emotional, and mental well-being. It is a necessary and vital aspect of self-care that can help individuals to feel more balanced, grounded, and resilient. When we practice self-care, we are better equipped to cope with the challenges and stresses of life, and to make positive choices for ourselves.

There are many different forms of self-care, and what works for one person may not be the same for another. Some common forms of self-care include:

Exercise and physical activity: Exercise and physical activity are important forms of self-care that can help to reduce stress, improve sleep, and boost mood. This may involve engaging in activities such as walking, running, swimming, or yoga.

Eating a healthy diet: A healthy diet is an important aspect of self-care, as it can help to support physical and mental well-being. This may involve incorporating a variety of nutrients and whole foods into one's diet, and avoiding processed or unhealthy foods.

Getting enough sleep: Sleep is an important form of self-care, as it is essential for physical and mental health. It is important to aim for 7-9 hours of sleep each night, and to create a sleep-friendly environment that is conducive to rest.

Taking breaks and relaxation: Taking breaks and relaxation are important forms of self-care that can help to reduce stress and improve well-being. This may involve activities such as reading, watching a movie, or taking a relaxing bath.

Seeking social support: Social support is an important form of self-care, as it can help to reduce feelings of isolation and loneliness, and can provide a sense of connection and belonging. This may involve seeking out supportive friends and family members, or joining a support group.

Practicing mindfulness: Mindfulness is a form of self-care that involves bringing one's attention to the present moment, and can help to reduce stress and improve well-being. This may involve activities such as meditation, deep breathing, or journaling.

By incorporating self-care activities into our lives, we can support our own healing and well-being, and feel more balanced and resilient. It is important to recognize that self-care is a necessary and vital aspect of our overall well-

being, and to prioritize it in our daily lives. It is also important to remember that self-care is not selfish, but rather it is an essential aspect of taking care of ourselves and being able to give back to others.

Self-care is particularly important during the healing process, as it can help to reduce stress and improve well-being. When we are healing from a difficult or traumatic experience, it is common to feel overwhelmed, exhausted, or drained. Self-care can help to nourish and restore us, and can provide a sense of comfort and support. It can also help to reduce feelings of anxiety or depression, and can improve our overall sense of well-being.

There are several steps that individuals can take to prioritize self-care during the healing process:

10: THE ROLE OF SELF-CARE IN THE HEALING PROCESS

– Identify your needs: The first step in prioritizing self-care during the healing process is to identify your own needs and what forms of self-care are most helpful for you. This may involve exploring your own values and what brings you joy and fulfillment, or seeking guidance from a therapist or other trusted resource.

– Set boundaries: Setting boundaries is an important aspect of self-care, as it helps to protect our own well-being and to feel more in control of our lives. Boundaries can be physical, emotional, or mental, and may involve setting limits on the types of interactions or behaviors that are acceptable, or setting limits on the amount of time and energy that is given to certain relationships or activities. By setting boundaries, we can feel more in control of our own lives and more able to take care of ourselves.

– Make self-care a priority: Once you have identified your needs and set boundaries, it is important to make self-care a priority in your daily life. This may involve setting aside dedicated time for self-care activities, or incorporating self-care into your daily routine. It is also important to be mindful of your own self-care needs and to prioritize them in your daily life.

– Seek support: Seeking support is an important aspect of self-care, and can be especially helpful during the healing process. This may involve seeking therapy or counseling, joining a support group, or seeking help from a trusted friend or family member. By seeking support, we can gain valuable perspective and guidance, and can feel more connected and less alone.

In conclusion, self-care is an important aspect of the healing process, and involves taking care of one's own physical, emotional, and mental well-being. By incorporating self-care activities into our lives, we can support our own healing and well-being, and feel more balanced and resilient. It is important to prioritize self-care, set boundaries, and seek support during the healing process. By taking these steps, individuals can further support their healing journey and improve their overall sense of well-being.

It is important to recognize that self-care looks different for everyone, and what works for one person may not be the same for another. It is important to be mindful of your own needs and to experiment with different forms of self-care to see what works best for you. It is also important to be kind to yourself and to recognize that it is okay to take breaks and to set limits when needed.

It is also important to be aware of any patterns of unhealthy or self-defeating behavior, and to seek help if needed. This may involve seeking therapy or counseling, or seeking help from a trusted friend or family member. By seeking help and support, individuals can work towards building healthy and supportive relationships that are based on respect and trust.

In conclusion, self-care is an important aspect of the healing process, and involves taking care of one's own physical, emotional, and mental well-being. It is a necessary and vital aspect of self-care that can help individuals to feel more balanced, grounded, and resilient. By incorporating self-care activities into our lives, setting boundaries, and seeking support, individuals can further support their healing journey and improve their overall sense of well-being.

11: Navigating Life After Gaslighting: Tips for Moving Forward

Navigating life after gaslighting can be a challenging and difficult process, as it involves rebuilding trust in oneself and one's own perceptions, and reclaiming control over one's own life and well-being. It is a process that may take time and effort, but with patience and persistence, it is possible to move forward in a positive direction.

There are several steps that individuals can take to navigate life after gaslighting and to move forward:

– Seek support: Seeking support is an important aspect of navigating life after gaslighting, as it can provide a sense of connection and belonging, and can help to reduce feelings of isolation and loneliness. This may involve seeking therapy or counseling, joining a support group, or seeking help from a trusted friend or family member. By seeking support, individuals can gain valuable perspective and guidance, and can feel more connected and less alone.

– Set boundaries: Setting boundaries is an important aspect of navigating life after gaslighting, as it helps to protect one's own well-being and to feel more in control of one's own life. Boundaries can be physical, emotional, or mental, and may involve setting limits on the types of interactions or behaviors that are acceptable, or setting limits on the amount of time and energy that is given to certain relationships or activities. By setting boundaries, individuals can feel more in control of their own lives and more able to take care of themselves.

– Practice self-care: Practicing self-care is an important aspect of navigating life after gaslighting, as it helps to reduce stress and improve well-being. Self-care can involve activities such as exercise, eating a healthy diet, getting enough sleep, and taking time for relaxation and leisure. By taking care of oneself, individuals can build resilience and feel more capable of handling challenges and setbacks.

– Learn to trust oneself: Trusting oneself is an important aspect of navigating life after gaslighting, as it involves rebuilding trust in one's own perceptions and experiences. This may involve learning to recognize and challenge negative self-talk, and working to develop a sense of self-acceptance and self-compassion. It is important to be patient with oneself and to recognize that rebuilding trust in oneself is a process that may take time.

– Seek out positive influences: Seeking out positive influences is an important aspect of navigating life after gaslighting, as it can help to provide a sense of support and encouragement. This may involve seeking out positive role models or seeking out supportive friends and family members. By seeking out positive influences, individuals can gain insight and inspiration, and can feel more motivated and supported.

– Set goals: Setting goals is an important aspect of navigating life after gaslighting, as it provides a sense of direction and helps to focus energy and efforts. Goals can be short-term or long-term, and can be related to various areas of one's life such as career, relationships, personal growth, or health and wellness. By setting goals and working towards their achievement, individuals can build a sense of accomplishment and self-worth.

In conclusion, navigating life after gaslighting can be a challenging and difficult process, but with patience and persistence, it is possible to move forward in a positive direction. By seeking support, setting boundaries, practicing self-care, learning to trust oneself, seeking out positive influences, and setting goals, individuals can navigate life after gaslighting and work towards rebuilding trust in oneself and reclaiming control over one's own life and well-being.

It is important to recognize that navigating life after gaslighting is a process that may involve challenges and setbacks, and it is important to be patient with oneself and to recognize that it is a journey. It is also important to be kind to oneself and to recognize that we are all human and that it is okay to make mistakes. By practicing self-compassion and by focusing on our strengths and accomplishments, we can build self-esteem and feel more positive and confident.

It is also important to be aware of negative self-talk and to challenge negative beliefs or thoughts that may be hindering our progress. Negative self-talk can be damaging to our self-esteem and can hold us back from achieving our goals. By recognizing and challenging negative self-talk, we can build a stronger sense of self-worth and confidence.

It is also important to be open to seeking support and resources if needed. This may involve seeking therapy or counseling, joining a support group, or seeking help from a trusted friend or family member. By seeking support, we can gain valuable perspective and guidance, and can build a stronger sense of self-worth and confidence.

In conclusion, navigating life after gaslighting is a process that involves seeking support, setting boundaries, practicing self-care, learning to trust oneself, seeking out positive influences, and setting goals. It is a process that may involve challenges and setbacks, and it is important to be patient with oneself and to recognize that it is a journey. By being kind to oneself, recognizing and challenging negative self-talk, and seeking support and resources if needed, individuals can navigate life after gaslighting and work towards rebuilding trust in oneself and reclaiming control over one's own life and well-being.

12: The Importance of Self-Compassion in Healing from Psychological Abuse

Self-compassion is an important aspect of healing from psychological abuse, as it involves treating oneself with kindness, understanding, and care, and recognizing that we are all human and that we all make mistakes. It is a powerful tool that can help individuals to heal from psychological abuse and to build a stronger sense of self-worth and confidence.

Self-compassion involves three core components: self-kindness, common humanity, and mindfulness.

– Self-kindness involves treating oneself with kindness and understanding, rather than with judgment or criticism. It involves being gentle and caring towards oneself, and recognizing that we all have flaws and limitations.

– Common humanity involves recognizing that suffering and struggles are a common part of the human experience, and that we are not alone in our experiences. It involves recognizing that we are all connected and that we all experience difficult emotions and challenges.

12: THE IMPORTANCE OF SELF-COMPASSION IN HEALING FROM PSYCHOLOGICAL ABUSE

– Mindfulness involves bringing awareness to the present moment and to our own thoughts and emotions without judgment. It involves accepting our experiences and emotions as they are, rather than trying to avoid or suppress them.

Self-compassion can be a powerful tool in healing from psychological abuse, as it helps to reduce feelings of shame and self-blame, and can help individuals to feel more accepting and understanding towards themselves. It can also help to reduce feelings of anxiety and depression, and can improve overall well-being.

There are several ways that individuals can practice self-compassion:

– Practice self-kindness: This may involve speaking to oneself in a kind and caring manner, or engaging in activities that bring joy and fulfillment.

– Remember that we are all human: This may involve reminding oneself that it is okay to make mistakes, and that we all have flaws and limitations.

12: THE IMPORTANCE OF SELF-COMPASSION IN HEALING FROM PSYCHOLOGICAL ABUSE

– Practice mindfulness: This may involve activities such as meditation, deep breathing, or journaling.

– Seek support: This may involve seeking therapy or counseling, joining a support group, or seeking help from a trusted friend or family member.

By practicing self-compassion, individuals can build a stronger sense of self-worth and confidence, and can feel more accepting and understanding towards themselves. It is an important aspect of healing from psychological abuse, and can help individuals to feel more resilient and capable of coping with challenges and setbacks.

It is important to recognize that practicing self-compassion is a process that may involve challenges and setbacks, and it is important to be patient with oneself and to recognize that it is a journey. It is also important to be kind to oneself and to recognize that we are all human and that it is okay to make mistakes. By focusing on our strengths and accomplishments, and by seeking support and resources if needed, we can build self-compassion and feel more positive and confident.

12: THE IMPORTANCE OF SELF-COMPASSION IN HEALING FROM PSYCHOLOGICAL ABUSE

In conclusion, self-compassion is an important aspect of healing from psychological abuse, and involves treating oneself with kindness, understanding, and care, and recognizing that we are all human and that we all make mistakes. It is a powerful tool that can help individuals to heal from psychological abuse and to build a stronger sense of self-worth and confidence. By practicing self-compassion, individuals can feel more accepting and understanding towards themselves, and can build resilience and feel more capable of coping with challenges and setbacks.

It is important to recognize that healing from psychological abuse is a process that may involve challenges and setbacks, and it is important to be patient with oneself and to recognize that it is a journey. It is also important to be kind to oneself and to recognize that it is okay to take breaks and to set limits when needed. By practicing self-compassion and by seeking support and resources if needed, individuals can further support their healing journey and build resilience and well-being.

It is also important to be aware of any patterns of unhealthy or self-defeating behavior, and to seek help if needed. This may involve seeking therapy or counseling, or seeking help from a trusted friend or family member. By seeking help and support, individuals can work towards building healthy and supportive relationships that are based on respect and trust.

In conclusion, healing from psychological abuse is a process that involves practicing self-compassion, seeking support, and being aware of any patterns of unhealthy or self-defeating behavior. It is a process that may involve challenges and setbacks, and it is important to be patient with oneself and to recognize that it is a journey. By being kind to oneself, seeking support and resources if needed, and working towards building healthy and supportive relationships, individuals can further support their healing journey and build resilience and well-being.

13: Finding Hope and Resilience After Gaslighting

Finding hope and resilience after gaslighting can be a challenging and difficult process, as it involves rebuilding trust in oneself and one's own perceptions, and reclaiming control over one's own life and well-being. It is a process that may take time and effort, but with patience and persistence, it is possible to find hope and resilience and to move forward in a positive direction.

There are several steps that individuals can take to find hope and resilience after gaslighting:

– Seek support: Seeking support is an important aspect of finding hope and resilience after gaslighting, as it can provide a sense of connection and belonging, and can help to reduce feelings of isolation and loneliness. This may involve seeking therapy or counseling, joining a support group, or seeking help from a trusted friend or family member. By seeking support, individuals can gain valuable perspective and guidance, and can feel more connected and less alone.

– Set boundaries: Setting boundaries is an important aspect

of finding hope and resilience after gaslighting, as it helps to protect one's own well-being and to feel more in control of one's own life. Boundaries can be physical, emotional, or mental, and may involve setting limits on the types of interactions or behaviors that are acceptable, or setting limits on the amount of time and energy that is given to certain relationships or activities. By setting boundaries, individuals can feel more in control of their own lives and more able to take care of themselves.

– Practice self-care: Practicing self-care is an important aspect of finding hope and resilience after gaslighting, as it helps to reduce stress and improve well-being. Self-care can involve activities such as exercise, eating a healthy diet, getting enough sleep, and taking time for relaxation and leisure. By taking care of oneself, individuals can build resilience and feel more capable of handling challenges and setbacks.

– Learn to trust oneself: Trusting oneself is an important aspect of finding hope and resilience after gaslighting, as it involves rebuilding trust in one's own perceptions and experiences. This may involve learning to recognize and challenge negative self-talk, and working to develop a sense of self-acceptance and self-compassion. It is important to be patient with oneself and to recognize that rebuilding trust in oneself is a process that may take time.

– Seek out positive influences: Seeking out positive influences is an important aspect of finding hope and resilience after gaslighting, as it can help to provide a sense of support and encouragement. This may involve seeking out positive role models or seeking out supportive friends and family members. By seeking out positive influences, individuals can gain insight and inspiration, and can feel more motivated and supported.

In conclusion, finding hope and resilience after gaslighting is a process that involves seeking support, setting boundaries, practicing self-care, learning to trust oneself, and seeking out positive influences. It is a process that may involve challenges and setbacks, and it is important to be patient with oneself and to recognize that it is a journey. By taking these steps, individuals can find hope and resilience after gaslighting and work towards rebuilding trust in oneself and reclaiming control over one's own life and well-being.

13: FINDING HOPE AND RESILIENCE AFTER GAS-LIGHTING

It is important to recognize that finding hope and resilience after gaslighting is a process that may involve challenges and setbacks, and it is important to be patient with oneself and to recognize that it is a journey. It is also important to be kind to oneself and to recognize that we are all human and that it is okay to make mistakes. By focusing on our strengths and accomplishments, and by seeking support and resources if needed, we can build hope and resilience and feel more positive and confident.

It is also important to be aware of negative self-talk and to challenge negative beliefs or thoughts that may be hindering our progress. Negative self-talk can be damaging to our self-esteem and can hold us back from achieving our goals. By recognizing and challenging negative self-talk, we can build a stronger sense of hope and resilience.

It is also important to be open to seeking support and resources if needed. This may involve seeking therapy or counseling, joining a support group, or seeking help from a trusted friend or family member. By seeking support, we can gain valuable perspective and guidance, and can build a stronger sense of hope and resilience.

13: FINDING HOPE AND RESILIENCE AFTER GAS-LIGHTING

In conclusion, finding hope and resilience after gaslighting is a process that involves seeking support, setting boundaries, practicing self-care, learning to trust oneself, and seeking out positive influences. It is a process that may involve challenges and setbacks, and it is important to be patient with oneself and to recognize that it is a journey. By being kind to oneself, recognizing and challenging negative self-talk, and seeking support and resources if needed, individuals can find hope and resilience after gaslighting and work towards rebuilding trust in oneself and reclaiming control over one's own life and well-being.

One way to find hope and resilience after gaslighting is to focus on small steps and progress, rather than on the overall journey. This can help to break the process down into manageable chunks, and can help to provide a sense of accomplishment and progress. It is important to be patient with oneself and to recognize that healing is a process that may take time, and to celebrate small victories along the way.

It is also important to remember that it is okay to feel a range of emotions, including anger, sadness, and frustration, and to allow oneself to feel and process these emo-

tions. By acknowledging and expressing these emotions, individuals can begin to heal and move forward.

It is also important to be mindful of self-care and to prioritize taking care of oneself. This may involve activities such as
exercise, eating a healthy diet, getting enough sleep, and
taking time for relaxation and leisure. By taking care of oneself, individuals can build resilience and feel more capable
of handling challenges and setbacks.

In conclusion, finding hope and resilience after gaslighting
is a process that involves seeking support, setting boundaries, practicing self-care, learning to trust oneself, and seeking out positive influences. It is a process that may involve
challenges and setbacks, and it is important to be patient
with oneself and to recognize that it is a journey. By focusing on small steps and progress, allowing oneself to feel and
process a range of emotions, and prioritizing self-care, individuals can find hope and resilience after gaslighting and
work towards rebuilding trust in oneself and reclaiming
control over one's own life and well-being.

Book 2 - Narcissistic Abuse

A Deep Dive into the Psychodynamics of Narcissistic Personality Disorder and Its Effects on the Self-Esteem, Well-Being, and Emotional Health of Those Who Have Suffered from Its Toxic Influence

01: What is Narcissistic Personality Disorder?

Narcissistic Personality Disorder (NPD) is a mental health condition characterized by an inflated sense of self-importance and a deep need for admiration. People with NPD often have a grandiose sense of their own capabilities and accomplishments, and they expect to be recognized as superior without having to meet the same standards as others.

At the core of NPD is a fragile ego that is easily threatened and prone to feelings of inadequacy. To protect themselves from these vulnerabilities, individuals with NPD may engage in a range of behaviors designed to boost their own ego and draw attention to themselves. These behaviors can include grandiose displays of wealth or success, manipulation of others, and a lack of empathy towards the feelings and needs of others.

NPD is classified as a "Cluster B" personality disorder, which means that it is characterized by dramatic and erratic behavior. Other personality disorders in this category include Borderline Personality Disorder, Antisocial Personality Disorder, and Histrionic Personality Disorder.

01: WHAT IS NARCISSISTIC PERSONALITY DISORDER?

Symptoms of NPD can be difficult to identify, as people with the disorder often present a highly favorable image of themselves to the world. However, common signs of NPD may include:

– An exaggerated sense of self-importance

– A preoccupation with fantasies of unlimited success, power, or attractiveness

– A belief that they are special and should only associate with other special or high-status people

– A need for excessive admiration and attention

– A lack of empathy towards others' feelings and needs

– Envy of others and a belief that others are envious of them

– Arrogant and haughty behavior

It is important to note that having some of these traits does not necessarily mean that someone has NPD. To be diagnosed with the disorder, a person must exhibit a significant number of these traits and have a pattern of behavior that is significantly different from what is considered normal in their cultural context.

NPD is often accompanied by other mental health conditions, such as depression, anxiety, and substance abuse disorders. It is also more common in men than in women.

The exact cause of NPD is not fully understood, but it is thought to be the result of a combination of genetic, environmental, and social factors. Some research suggests that people who have experienced childhood abuse or neglect may be more at risk of developing NPD later in life.

Treatment for NPD typically involves a combination of psychotherapy and medication. Psychotherapy, such as cognitive-behavioral therapy (CBT), can help individuals with NPD learn to recognize and change their unhealthy patterns of thinking and behavior. Medications, such as selective serotonin reuptake inhibitors (SSRIs), may be used to treat any accompanying mental health conditions, such as depression or anxiety.

It is important to note that NPD can be a difficult condition to treat, as individuals with the disorder may not recognize that they have a problem and may resist treatment. It is also common for people with NPD to have difficulty maintaining relationships and may struggle with social isolation as a result of their behavior.

In conclusion, Narcissistic Personality Disorder is a mental health condition characterized by an inflated sense of self-importance and a deep need for admiration. It is characterized by a range of behaviors designed to boost the individual's ego and draw attention to themselves, and is often accompanied by other mental health conditions. While it can be a challenging condition to treat, a combination of psychotherapy and medication can be effective in helping individuals with NPD learn to recognize and change their unhealthy patterns of thinking and behavior.

It is important to recognize that not all narcissistic behavior is indicative of NPD. It is common for people to have some narcissistic traits, and it is only when these traits become extreme and dysfunctional that they may be indicative of a personality disorder.

It is also important to recognize that people with NPD are not necessarily "bad" or malevolent. Many people with NPD may not be aware of the impact their behavior has on others and may not understand the pain and suffering they cause. With proper treatment, individuals with NPD can learn to recognize and change their unhealthy patterns of behavior and develop healthier, more fulfilling relationships.

It is also important for loved ones of individuals with NPD to seek support and take care of their own well-being. Dealing with someone with NPD can be emotionally draining and can take a toll on one's own mental health. It is important to set boundaries, practice self-care, and seek support from friends, family, or a therapist if needed.

In summary, Narcissistic Personality Disorder is a complex and often misunderstood mental health condition that can have a significant impact on the lives of those affected by it. It is important to recognize the signs of NPD and seek treatment if necessary in order to improve the well-being and relationships of those affected by the disorder.

It is also important for individuals who have experienced narcissistic abuse to seek support and seek help in healing from the trauma. Narcissistic abuse can have serious consequences for one's emotional well-being and can leave a person feeling confused, isolated, and lacking in self-worth.

Therapy can be a helpful resource for individuals who have experienced narcissistic abuse, as it can provide a safe and supportive space to process and work through the trauma. It can also be helpful to join a support group or connect with others who have experienced similar abuse, as it can provide a sense of community and understanding.

It is also important to remember that healing from narcissistic abuse takes time, and it is important to be patient with oneself and to practice self-care. This can include activities such as exercise, meditation, and engaging in activities that bring joy and relaxation.

In conclusion, it is important to recognize the serious impact that narcissistic abuse can have on one's emotional health and well-being. It is important to seek support and treatment in order to heal from the trauma and build a healthy and fulfilling life.

It is also important for individuals to educate themselves about narcissistic abuse and the dynamics of narcissistic relationships. Understanding the patterns of behavior and the tactics that narcissists use can help individuals recognize abusive behavior and take steps to protect themselves from it.

It is also important to remember that not all narcissists are the same, and the behaviors and tactics that they use can vary. Some narcissists may be more overt and aggressive in their abuse, while others may be more subtle and manipulative.

It is also important to recognize that not all relationships with narcissists have to be toxic. With proper boundaries, communication, and self-care, it is possible to have a relationship with a narcissist that is functional and healthy.

In conclusion, it is important for individuals to educate themselves about narcissistic abuse and to take steps to protect themselves from it. It is also important to recognize that healing from narcissistic abuse takes time and to be patient with oneself during the healing process. With proper support and treatment, it is possible to build a healthy and fulfilling life after experiencing narcissistic abuse.

02: The Characteristics of Nar-cissistic Abuse

Narcissistic abuse is a form of psychological abuse that is characterized by a pattern of manipulation, control, and exploitation in a relationship. It is often perpetrated by individuals with Narcissistic Personality Disorder (NPD), although not all narcissists engage in abusive behavior.

One of the defining characteristics of narcissistic abuse is that it is covert and insidious. Narcissists are often skilled at hiding their abusive behavior and may even present a charming and likable exterior to the world. This can make it difficult for victims of narcissistic abuse to recognize that they are being abused and to seek help.

There are a range of tactics that narcissists may use in order to maintain control and manipulate their victims. These tactics can include:

– Gaslighting: This refers to the act of manipulating someone into doubting their own perceptions and memories. A narcissist may deny that certain events occurred, or they may manipulate evidence in order to make their victim question their own recollection of events.

– Triangulation: This involves bringing a third party into the dynamic of the relationship in order to create jealousy and insecurity in the victim. A narcissist may flirt with other people in front of their victim or compare their victim to others in order to undermine their self-esteem.

– Love bombing: This involves showering the victim with excessive attention, affection, and gifts in the early stages of the relationship in order to create an intense bond. This can make it difficult for the victim to leave the relationship later on.

– Isolation: A narcissist may try to isolate their victim from friends and family in order to increase their dependence on the narcissist and to make it more difficult for the victim to seek support.

– Economic abuse: A narcissist may control their victim's access to financial resources in order to maintain control over the victim. This can include withholding money, controlling how the victim spends money, or preventing the victim from working.

– Emotional abuse: Narcissists may use a range of tactics to emotionally abuse their victims, including belittling, criticizing, and mocking their victim's feelings and needs. They may also use emotional blackmail in order to get their victim to do what they want, such as threatening to harm themselves if their victim does not comply.

– Physical abuse: While not all narcissists engage in physical abuse, some may use physical violence as a means of control. This can include hitting, pushing, or restraining their victim.

One of the most damaging aspects of narcissistic abuse is the way it can erode the victim's sense of self-worth and identity. Narcissists may use a range of tactics to chip away at their victim's self-esteem, including criticism, belittling, and manipulation. This can leave the victim feeling confused, isolated, and unsure of their own perceptions and feelings.

It is important to recognize that narcissistic abuse can have serious consequences for the mental health and well-being of the victim. It can lead to anxiety, depression, and post-traumatic stress disorder (PTSD). It is also common for victims of narcissistic abuse to develop a sense of learned helplessness, in which they feel unable to make decisions or take action on their own.

If you suspect that you or someone you know is experiencing narcissistic abuse, it is important to seek help. This can include talking to a therapist or counselor, reaching out to a support group, or contacting a domestic violence hotline for guidance and support.

In conclusion, narcissistic abuse is a form of psychological abuse that is characterized by a pattern of manipulation and control. It can have serious consequences for the mental health and well-being of the victim, and it is important to seek help if you suspect that you or someone you know is experiencing this type of abuse.

It is also important for individuals who have experienced narcissistic abuse to remember that they are not alone and that they are not to blame for the abuse they have suffered. It can be easy for victims of narcissistic abuse to internalize the blame and to believe that they are responsible for the abuse. It is important to recognize that the abuse is not the victim's fault and that they have the right to seek help and to create a healthy and fulfilling life for themselves.

It is also important for individuals who have experienced

narcissistic abuse to work on rebuilding their sense of self and their self-worth. This can be a difficult process, but it is an essential step in the healing journey. Therapy can be a helpful resource in this process, as can connecting with others who have experienced similar abuse.

It is also important to set boundaries and to learn to assert oneself in healthy ways. This can include learning how to say no, setting limits on what is acceptable behavior, and seeking support when needed.

In conclusion, recovering from narcissistic abuse is a process that takes time and effort. It is important to seek help, to work on rebuilding a sense of self, and to set boundaries in order to create a healthy and fulfilling life. With the right support and resources, it is possible to heal from the trauma of narcissistic abuse and to create a life that is fulfilling and satisfying.

It is also important for individuals who have experienced narcissistic abuse to remember that healing is a journey and that it is okay to take things one step at a time. It is important to be patient with oneself and to recognize that it is normal to have setbacks and difficult days.

It is also important to have self-compassion and to treat oneself with kindness and understanding. This can be especially difficult for individuals who have experienced narcissistic abuse, as their sense of self-worth may have been severely damaged. It is important to remind oneself that it is okay to make mistakes and that it is possible to learn from them and grow.

It is also important to focus on self-care and to prioritize one's own well-being. This can include activities such as exercise, meditation, and engaging in hobbies and activities that bring joy and relaxation. It is also important to make time for self-care and to prioritize it as a regular part of one's routine.

In conclusion, healing from narcissistic abuse is a journey that takes time and effort. It is important to be patient with oneself, to have self-compassion, and to prioritize self-care in order to create a healthy and fulfilling life. With the right support and resources, it is possible to heal from the trauma of narcissistic abuse and to create a life that is fulfilling and satisfying.

03: The Impact of Narcissistic Abuse on the Self-Esteem

The impact of narcissistic abuse on the self-esteem of the victim can be profound and long-lasting. Narcissistic abuse is characterized by a pattern of manipulation, control, and exploitation, and it can erode the victim's sense of self-worth and identity.

One of the defining characteristics of narcissistic abuse is that it is covert and insidious. Narcissists are often skilled at hiding their abusive behavior and may even present a charming and likable exterior to the world. This can make it difficult for victims of narcissistic abuse to recognize that they are being abused and to seek help.

The tactics that narcissists use in order to manipulate and control their victims can include gaslighting, triangulation, love bombing, isolation, economic abuse, emotional abuse, and physical abuse. These tactics can leave the victim feeling confused, isolated, and unsure of their own perceptions and feelings.

One of the most damaging aspects of narcissistic abuse is the way it can erode the victim's sense of self-worth and identity. Narcissists may use a range of tactics to chip away at their victim's self-esteem, including criticism, belittling, and manipulation. This can leave the victim feeling inadequate and unsure of their own value.

It is common for victims of narcissistic abuse to develop a sense of learned helplessness, in which they feel unable to make decisions or take action on their own. They may also develop a range of negative beliefs about themselves, such as believing that they are unworthy, defective, or unlovable. These negative beliefs can become deeply ingrained and can have a serious impact on the victim's self-esteem.

The impact of narcissistic abuse on the self-esteem of the victim can also extend to their relationships with others. Victims of narcissistic abuse may struggle to trust others and may have difficulty forming and maintaining healthy relationships. They may also have a difficult time setting boundaries and may struggle to assert themselves in healthy ways.

It is important to recognize that the impact of narcissistic abuse on the self-esteem of the victim can be long-lasting and can extend to other areas of their life. It can affect their mental health, their relationships, and their overall sense of well-being.

It is also important to recognize that the effects of narcissistic abuse can be healed and that it is possible to rebuild a healthy sense of self-worth and identity. Therapy can be a helpful resource in this process, as can connecting with others who have experienced similar abuse. It is also important to set boundaries, to learn to assert oneself in healthy ways, and to practice self-care in order to rebuild a healthy sense of self.

In conclusion, the impact of narcissistic abuse on the self-esteem of the victim can be profound and long-lasting. It can affect their mental health, their relationships, and their overall sense of well-being. However, it is possible to heal from the effects of narcissistic abuse and to rebuild a healthy sense of self-worth and identity with the right support and resources.

It is also important for individuals who have experienced narcissistic abuse to recognize that healing is a journey and that it is okay to take things one step at a time. It is important to be patient with oneself and to recognize that it is normal to have setbacks and difficult days.

It is also important to have self-compassion and to treat oneself with kindness and understanding. This can be especially difficult for individuals who have experienced narcissistic abuse, as their sense of self-worth may have been severely damaged. It is important to remind oneself that it is okay to make mistakes and that it is possible to learn from them and grow.

One way to practice self-compassion is through the use of affirmations. Affirmations are positive statements that can help to shift negative thought patterns and to rebuild a healthy sense of self-worth. Examples of affirmations that may be helpful for individuals who have experienced narcissistic abuse include:

– "I am worthy of love and respect."

– "I am deserving of healthy and fulfilling relationships."

– "I am capable of setting boundaries and taking care of myself."

– "I am enough just as I am."

03: THE IMPACT OF NARCISSISTIC ABUSE ON THE SELF-ESTEEM

It is also important to focus on self-care and to prioritize one's own well-being. This can include activities such as exercise, meditation, and engaging in hobbies and activities that bring joy and relaxation. It is also important to make time for self-care and to prioritize it as a regular part of one's routine.

In conclusion, healing from the impact of narcissistic abuse on the self-esteem is a journey that takes time and effort. It is important to be patient with oneself, to have self-compassion, and to prioritize self-care in order to rebuild a healthy sense of self-worth. With the right support and resources, it is possible to heal from the trauma of narcissistic abuse and to create a life that is fulfilling and satisfying.

It is also important for individuals who have experienced narcissistic abuse to recognize that they are not alone and that they are not to blame for the abuse they have suffered. It can be easy for victims of narcissistic abuse to internalize the blame and to believe that they are responsible for the abuse. It is important to recognize that the abuse is not the victim's fault and that they have the right to seek help and to create a healthy and fulfilling life for themselves.

It is also important to reach out for support. This can include talking to a therapist or counselor, reaching out to a support group, or contacting a domestic violence hotline for guidance and support. It can be helpful to connect with others who have experienced similar abuse, as it can provide a sense of understanding and community.

It is also important to remember that healing from narcissistic abuse takes time and that it is normal to have ups and downs in the process. It is important to be patient with oneself and to recognize that it is okay to take things one step at a time.

In conclusion, it is important for individuals who have experienced narcissistic abuse to recognize that they are not alone and that they are not to blame for the abuse they have suffered. It is important to seek support, to reach out for help, and to be patient with oneself in the healing process. With the right support and resources, it is possible to heal from the trauma of narcissistic abuse and to create a healthy and fulfilling life.

It is also important for individuals who have experienced narcissistic abuse to work on rebuilding their sense of self and their self-worth. This can be a difficult process, but it is an essential step in the healing journey. Therapy can be a helpful resource in this process, as can connecting with others who have experienced similar abuse.

One way to work on rebuilding a healthy sense of self is through the use of affirmations and positive self-talk. It can be helpful to write down affirmations and to repeat them to oneself on a daily basis. This can help to shift negative thought patterns and to rebuild a healthy sense of self-worth.

It can also be helpful to engage in activities that help to build self-esteem and to develop a sense of accomplishment. This can include setting and working towards goals, learning new skills, and participating in activities that bring joy and satisfaction.

It is also important to set boundaries and to learn to assert oneself in healthy ways. This can include learning how to say no, setting limits on what is acceptable behavior, and seeking support when needed. Setting boundaries is an important way to take care of oneself and to ensure that one's own needs and well-being are being met.

03: THE IMPACT OF NARCISSISTIC ABUSE ON THE SELF-ESTEEM

In conclusion, rebuilding a healthy sense of self and self-worth is an important part of the healing process after experiencing narcissistic abuse. It is important to engage in activities that help to build self-esteem, to set boundaries, and to practice self-care in order to rebuild a healthy sense of self. With the right support and resources, it is possible to heal from the trauma of narcissistic abuse and to create a life that is fulfilling and satisfying.

04: The Effects of Narcissistic Abuse on Emotional Health

The effects of narcissistic abuse on emotional health can be profound and long-lasting. Narcissistic abuse is characterized by a pattern of manipulation, control, and exploitation, and it can have serious consequences for the mental health of the victim.

One of the defining characteristics of narcissistic abuse is that it is covert and insidious. Narcissists are often skilled at hiding their abusive behavior and may even present a charming and likable exterior to the world. This can make it difficult for victims of narcissistic abuse to recognize that they are being abused and to seek help.

The tactics that narcissists use in order to manipulate and control their victims can include gaslighting, triangulation, love bombing, isolation, economic abuse, emotional abuse, and physical abuse. These tactics can leave the victim feeling confused, isolated, and unsure of their own perceptions and feelings.

One of the most damaging aspects of narcissistic abuse is the way it can affect the emotional health of the victim. It can lead to a range of mental health issues, including anxiety, depression, and post-traumatic stress disorder (PTSD).

Victims of narcissistic abuse may also struggle with emotional regulation and may have difficulty managing their emotions in a healthy way. They may have a tendency to suppress their emotions or to act out in unhealthy ways, such as lashing out at others or engaging in self-destructive behaviors.

It is important to recognize that the effects of narcissistic abuse on emotional health can be long-lasting and can extend to other areas of the victim's life. It can affect their relationships, their work, and their overall sense of well-being.

It is also important to recognize that the effects of narcissistic abuse on emotional health can be healed and that it is possible to rebuild a healthy emotional foundation. Therapy can be a helpful resource in this process, as can connecting with others who have experienced similar abuse. It is also important to practice self-care and to prioritize one's own well-being in order to rebuild emotional health.

In conclusion, the effects of narcissistic abuse on emotional health can be profound and long-lasting. It can lead to a range of mental health issues and can affect the victim's relationships, work, and overall sense of well-being. However, it is possible to heal from the effects of narcissistic abuse and to rebuild a healthy emotional foundation with the right support and resources.

It is also important for individuals who have experienced narcissistic abuse to seek support and to reach out for help. This can include talking to a therapist or counselor, reaching out to a support group, or contacting a domestic violence hotline for guidance and support. It can be helpful to connect with others who have experienced similar abuse, as it can provide a sense of understanding and community.

One way to work on rebuilding trust is through the use of affirmations and positive self-talk. It can be helpful to write down affirmations and to repeat them to oneself on a daily basis. This can help to shift negative thought patterns and to rebuild a healthy sense of trust in oneself.

It is also important to remember that healing from narcissistic abuse takes time and that it is normal to have ups and downs in the process. It is important to be patient with one-self and to recognize that it is okay to take things one step at a time.

It is also important to set boundaries and to learn to assert oneself in healthy ways. This can include learning how to say no, setting limits on what is acceptable behavior, and seeking support when needed. Setting boundaries is an important way to take care of oneself and to ensure that one's own needs and well-being are being met.

In conclusion, it is important for individuals who have experienced narcissistic abuse to seek support, to reach out for help, and to set boundaries in order to rebuild emotional health. It is important to be patient with oneself and to recognize that healing is a journey that takes time. With the right support and resources, it is possible to heal from the trauma of narcissistic abuse and to create a healthy and fulfilling life.

It is also important for individuals who have experienced narcissistic abuse to work on rebuilding their relationships with others. Narcissistic abuse can damage the victim's relationships with others and can make it difficult for them to trust and connect with others in a healthy way.

One way to work on rebuilding relationships is through the use of effective communication skills. This can include learning how to express one's needs and boundaries in a healthy way, listening actively to others, and being open and honest in communication.

It can also be helpful to engage in activities that help to build social connections and to develop a sense of community. This can include joining a support group, participating in hobbies and activities that bring joy and satisfaction, and volunteering in the community.

It is also important to set boundaries and to learn to assert oneself in healthy ways. This can include learning how to say no, setting limits on what is acceptable behavior, and seeking support when needed. Setting boundaries is an important way to take care of oneself and to ensure that one's own needs and well-being are being met.

In conclusion, rebuilding relationships with others is an important part of the healing process after experiencing narcissistic abuse. It is important to learn effective communication skills, to engage in activities that help to build social connections, and to set boundaries in order to rebuild healthy relationships. With the right support and resources, it is possible to heal from the trauma of narcissistic abuse and to create a healthy and fulfilling life.

05: The Dynamics of Narcissistic Relationships

The dynamics of narcissistic relationships are complex and can be difficult to understand. Narcissistic personality disorder is a mental health condition characterized by an inflated sense of self-importance, a need for admiration, and a lack of empathy for others. Narcissistic individuals may have a grandiose sense of self and may see themselves as superior to others.

In relationships, narcissists may use their charisma and charm to manipulate and control their partners. They may also engage in abusive behaviors, such as gaslighting, triangulation, love bombing, isolation, economic abuse, emotional abuse, and physical abuse. These tactics can leave the victim feeling confused, isolated, and unsure of their own perceptions and feelings.

One of the most challenging aspects of narcissistic relationships is the way that narcissists can change their behavior in order to manipulate their partners. They may be charming and loving at one moment and then turn cold and dismissive the next. This can make it difficult for the victim to trust their own perceptions and to understand what is happening in the relationship.

Narcissists may also engage in "love bombing," which is a tactic in which they shower their partners with affection and attention in the beginning stages of the relationship in order to win their trust and affection. This can be especially confusing for the victim, as it can make it difficult for them to see the narcissist's true intentions.

It is important to recognize that narcissistic relationships are not healthy and that they can have serious consequences for the victim's emotional and mental health. If you are in a narcissistic relationship, it is important to seek help and to get out of the relationship as soon as possible.

In conclusion, the dynamics of narcissistic relationships are complex and can be difficult to understand. Narcissistic individuals may use manipulation and abuse in order to control their partners and may engage in "love bombing" in the beginning stages of the relationship. It is important to recognize that narcissistic relationships are not healthy and to seek help if you are in one.

It is important to remember that leaving a narcissistic relationship can be challenging and that it may take time and effort. It is important to have a plan in place and to reach out for support from trusted friends, family, or a therapist.

It is also important to recognize that the victim of narcissistic abuse is not to blame for the abuse they have suffered. Narcissistic individuals are responsible for their own behavior and for the harm they have caused.

It is also important to take care of oneself and to prioritize one's own well-being after leaving a narcissistic relationship. This can include seeking therapy, practicing self-care, and setting boundaries to ensure that one's own needs are being met.

It is also important to recognize that healing from narcissistic abuse takes time and that it is normal to have ups and downs in the process. It is important to be patient with oneself and to recognize that it is okay to take things one step at a time.

In conclusion, leaving a narcissistic relationship can be challenging but it is an important step in the healing process. It is important to have a plan in place, to reach out for support, and to prioritize one's own well-being in order to rebuild a healthy and fulfilling life. It is also important to recognize that healing takes time and to be patient with oneself in the process.

It is important to remember that leaving a narcissistic relationship can be challenging and that it may take time and effort. It is important to have a plan in place and to reach out for support from trusted friends, family, or a therapist.

It is also important to recognize that the victim of narcissistic abuse is not to blame for the abuse they have suffered. Narcissistic individuals are responsible for their own behavior and for the harm they have caused.

It is also important to take care of oneself and to prioritize one's own well-being after leaving a narcissistic relationship. This can include seeking therapy, practicing self-care, and setting boundaries to ensure that one's own needs are being met.

It is also important to recognize that healing from narcissistic abuse takes time and that it is normal to have ups and downs in the process. It is important to be patient with oneself and to recognize that it is okay to take things one step at a time.

In conclusion, leaving a narcissistic relationship can be challenging but it is an important step in the healing process. It is important to have a plan in place, to reach out for support, and to prioritize one's own well-being in order to rebuild a healthy and fulfilling life. It is also important to recognize that healing takes time and to be patient with oneself in the process.

It is also important to recognize that healing from narcissistic abuse is a journey and that it is okay to take things one step at a time. It is important to be patient with oneself and to recognize that it is normal to have setbacks and difficult days.

It is also important to have self-compassion and to treat oneself with kindness and understanding. This can be especially difficult for individuals who have experienced narcissistic abuse, as their sense of self-worth may have been severely damaged. It is important to remind oneself that it is okay to make mistakes and that it is possible to learn from them and grow.

It is also important for individuals who have experienced narcissistic abuse to work on rebuilding their sense of trust and to learn to trust themselves again. Narcissistic abuse can shatter the victim's sense of trust in themselves and in others, and it can be difficult to rebuild this trust.

One way to work on rebuilding trust is through the use of affirmations and positive self-talk. It can be helpful to write down affirmations and to repeat them to oneself on a daily basis. This can help to shift negative thought patterns and to rebuild a healthy sense of trust in oneself.

It can also be helpful to engage in activities that help to build self-esteem and to develop a sense of accomplishment. This can include setting and working towards goals, learning new skills, and participating in activities that bring joy and satisfaction.

It is also important to set boundaries and to learn to assert oneself in healthy ways. This can include learning how to say no, setting limits on what is acceptable behavior, and seeking support when needed. Setting boundaries is an important way to take care of oneself and to ensure that one's own needs and well-being are being met.

In conclusion, rebuilding trust in oneself and in others is an important part of the healing process after experiencing narcissistic abuse. It is important to engage in activities that help to build self-esteem, to set boundaries, and to practice self-care in order to rebuild trust. With the right support and resources, it is possible to heal from the trauma of narcissistic abuse and to create a healthy and fulfilling life.

06: The Cycle of Narcissistic Abuse

The Cycle of Narcissistic Abuse is a term that describes the way in which narcissistic individuals and their relationships progress. It is not uncommon for victims of narcissistic abuse to feel confused and unsure of what is happening to them, and the cycle of abuse can be difficult to identify and understand. However, understanding this cycle can be an important step in breaking free from an abusive relationship and seeking help.

The cycle of narcissistic abuse begins with the "idealization" phase. In this phase, the narcissistic individual puts their partner on a pedestal, showering them with affection, attention, and flattery. They may promise their partner the world and make them feel special and loved. This phase can be intoxicating and can make the victim feel like they have found their perfect match.

However, the idealization phase is often short-lived, and it is eventually followed by the "devaluation" phase. In this phase, the narcissistic individual begins to tear down their partner and chip away at their self-esteem. They may criticize their partner's appearance, intelligence, or accomplishments, and they may belittle or dismiss their thoughts and feelings. They may also start to distance themselves emotionally, becoming cold and distant.

The victim of narcissistic abuse may try to please their partner and work to win back their love and affection during the devaluation phase. However, their efforts are often in vain, as the narcissistic individual is not capable of feeling genuine love or empathy.

The cycle of abuse is often followed by the "discard" phase, in which the narcissistic individual abruptly ends the relationship, leaving their partner heartbroken and confused. They may move on to a new partner and repeat the cycle, or they may simply move on without a replacement.

The victim of narcissistic abuse may feel a sense of relief upon the end of the relationship, but the emotional and psychological effects of the abuse can linger long after the relationship is over. They may struggle with feelings of worthlessness, self-doubt, and depression. They may also have difficulty trusting others and forming healthy relationships in the future.

It is important for victims of narcissistic abuse to seek help and support in order to heal and move on from the abuse. This may involve seeking therapy, joining a support group, or finding other resources to help them cope with the effects of the abuse.

It is also important for individuals to be aware of the signs of narcissistic abuse and to be cautious about entering into relationships with narcissistic individuals. Some warning signs of narcissistic abuse include a lack of empathy, a sense of entitlement, and an exaggerated sense of self-importance. It is also common for narcissistic individuals to manipulate and control their partners, and to use emotional abuse as a means of maintaining power and control in the relationship.

Breaking free from the cycle of narcissistic abuse can be a difficult and challenging process, but it is possible with the right support and resources. By seeking help and learning to recognize and avoid abusive relationships, individuals can take control of their lives and work towards a brighter, healthier future.

It is important to note that not all narcissistic individuals will follow the exact same cycle of abuse, and the length and intensity of each phase can vary. Some narcissistic individuals may remain in the idealization phase for longer periods of time, while others may move quickly through the cycle.

In some cases, the cycle of narcissistic abuse may involve "hoovering," in which the narcissistic individual tries to win back their partner after a period of abuse or abandonment. They may use tactics such as apologizing, promising to change, or showering their partner with attention and gifts in an attempt to regain their love and loyalty.

It is important for victims of narcissistic abuse to be aware of these tactics and to recognize that the narcissistic individual is not truly remorseful or committed to change. It is also important for victims to remember that they deserve love and respect, and to set boundaries and establish strict limits with their narcissistic partner.

Leaving a narcissistic relationship can be difficult, and it may involve facing intimidation, threats, and other forms of manipulation. It is important for victims to have a plan in place and to seek support from trusted friends, family members, or a domestic violence hotline.

Recovering from narcissistic abuse can be a long and difficult process, but it is possible with the right help and support. It is important for victims to take care of themselves and to prioritize their own well-being. This may involve seeking therapy, joining a support group, or finding other resources to help them cope with the effects of the abuse.

It is also important for individuals to educate themselves about narcissistic abuse and to be aware of the signs and dynamics of this type of abuse. By understanding the cycle of narcissistic abuse and learning to recognize and avoid abusive relationships, individuals can take control of their lives and work towards a brighter, healthier future.

In addition to seeking help and support, it is important for victims of narcissistic abuse to work on rebuilding their self-esteem and sense of worth. Narcissistic individuals often seek out and target individuals who are already struggling with self-doubt and low self-esteem, as they are more likely to be manipulated and controlled.

Victims of narcissistic abuse may benefit from activities and techniques that help to improve their self-esteem, such as positive affirmations, self-care practices, and setting and achieving personal goals. It can also be helpful to surround oneself with supportive and nurturing individuals who can provide love and encouragement.

It is also important for victims to recognize that the abuse they experienced was not their fault, and that they are not to blame for the behavior of their narcissistic partner. It can be helpful to work with a therapist or other mental health professional to process the abuse and to learn to let go of any feelings of responsibility or self-blame.

It can be challenging to move on and heal after experiencing narcissistic abuse, but it is possible with the right help and support. It is important for victims to remember that they are not alone, and that there are resources and support available to help them heal and rebuild their lives. With time, patience, and self-care, individuals can learn to let go of the past and move forward towards a brighter and healthier future.

In addition to seeking therapy and support from trusted individuals, there are a number of other steps that individuals can take to help them heal and recover from narcissistic abuse. Some additional tips for recovering from narcissistic abuse include:

− Practice self-care: It is important to prioritize self-care and to engage in activities that nourish and support your physical, emotional, and mental well-being. This may involve getting enough sleep, eating a healthy diet, exercising, and engaging in activities that bring joy and relaxation.

– Set boundaries: It is important to set clear boundaries with the narcissistic individual and to communicate your needs and limits to them. This may involve cutting off contact or limiting communication to specific times or places.

– Build a support system: Surrounding yourself with supportive and caring individuals can be a powerful tool in your recovery. Seek out friends and family members who can provide love, encouragement, and a listening ear. You may also consider joining a support group or connecting with other individuals who have experienced narcissistic abuse.

– Learn to recognize manipulation: Narcissistic individuals often use manipulation as a means of controlling and manipulating their partners. It is important to be aware of common manipulative tactics, such as gaslighting, love bombing, and triangulation, and to be prepared to stand up for yourself and set boundaries if these tactics are used against you.

– Seek professional help: Working with a therapist or other mental health professional can be a powerful tool in your recovery from narcissistic abuse. A therapist can help you process your experiences, work through your emotions, and develop coping strategies to deal with the aftermath of the abuse.

By following these tips and seeking help and support, individuals can take important steps towards healing and recovery from narcissistic abuse. With time and patience, it is possible to break free from the cycle of abuse and to build a brighter and healthier future.

It is important to note that recovery from narcissistic abuse is not a linear process, and it is common for individuals to experience setbacks and challenges along the way. It is normal to feel a range of emotions, including anger, sadness, fear, and confusion, and it is important to allow yourself the time and space to process these emotions.

It may also be helpful to remind yourself that the abuse was not your fault, and that you deserve love and respect. It can be helpful to work with a therapist or other mental health professional to help you work through any feelings of self-blame or guilt.

Another important aspect of recovery from narcissistic abuse is learning to establish healthy boundaries and to communicate effectively. Narcissistic individuals often rely on manipulation and control to maintain power in the relationship, and it is important to learn how to assert yourself and set clear limits with others.

It may also be helpful to practice self-compassion and to be kind and understanding towards yourself as you navigate the recovery process. It can be easy to fall into negative self-talk or to be overly critical of yourself, but it is important to remember that you are doing the best you can and that you deserve love and care.

Finally, it is important to remember that recovery is a journey, and that it may take time to heal and move on from the abuse. It is okay to take things one step at a time and to be patient with yourself as you work towards healing and recovery. With the right help and support, it is possible to break free from the cycle of narcissistic abuse and to build a brighter and healthier future.

07: The Trauma of Narcissistic Abuse

The trauma of narcissistic abuse can be deep and long-lasting, leaving victims feeling isolated, confused, and unsure of how to move forward. Narcissistic individuals often use manipulation, control, and emotional abuse as a means of maintaining power and control in the relationship, and the effects of this abuse can be devastating.

One of the most common forms of narcissistic abuse is gaslighting, which involves manipulating a victim into doubting their own perceptions and memories. The narcissistic individual may deny certain events or conversations took place, or they may twist the truth in order to make the victim feel confused and unsure of what is real. This can be extremely disorienting and can cause the victim to question their own sanity.

Another common form of narcissistic abuse is love bombing, in which the narcissistic individual showers their partner with excessive amounts of attention and affection in the beginning stages of the relationship. This can be intoxicating for the victim, who may feel like they have found their perfect match. However, this phase is often short-lived, and it is followed by a period of devaluation in which the narcissistic individual begins to tear down their partner and chip away at their self-esteem.

The trauma of narcissistic abuse can have a profound impact on a victim's emotional and psychological well-being. They may struggle with feelings of worthlessness, self-doubt, and depression. They may also have difficulty trusting others and forming healthy relationships in the future.

The effects of narcissistic abuse can also extend to a victim's physical health. Stress and anxiety, common responses to abuse, can have a range of physical symptoms, including insomnia, headaches, and stomach problems. The constant emotional rollercoaster of an abusive relationship can also take a toll on the immune system, making individuals more susceptible to illness.

It is important for victims of narcissistic abuse to seek help and support in order to heal and move on from the trauma. This may involve seeking therapy, joining a support group, or finding other resources to help them cope with the effects of the abuse. It is also important for victims to practice self-care and to prioritize their own well-being as they work towards recovery.

It is important to recognize that recovery from narcissistic abuse is a process and that it may take time to heal and move on from the trauma. It is normal to experience set-backs and challenges along the way, and it is important to be patient with oneself and to allow oneself the time and space to process and heal.

By seeking help and support, practicing self-care, and set-ting boundaries, victims of narcissistic abuse can take im-portant steps towards healing and recovery. With time and patience, it is possible to break free from the cycle of abuse and to build a brighter, healthier future.

It is important for victims of narcissistic abuse to under-stand that the trauma they have experienced is real and that it is not their fault. Narcissistic individuals are often skilled at manipulating and controlling their partners, and they may use tactics such as gaslighting and love bombing to confuse and disorient their victims.

It can be helpful for victims to educate themselves about narcissistic abuse and to learn about the common tactics that narcissistic individuals use. This can help them to recognize when they are being manipulated or controlled, and to take steps to protect themselves and set boundaries.

It is also important for victims of narcissistic abuse to seek support and validation from trusted friends, family members, or a therapist. It can be easy to feel isolated and alone after experiencing abuse, and having a supportive network of people can be crucial in the recovery process.

Another important aspect of recovery from the trauma of narcissistic abuse is learning to practice self-compassion and to be kind and understanding towards oneself. It is common for victims of abuse to struggle with feelings of self-blame and to be overly critical of themselves. It is important to remember that the abuse was not your fault, and that you deserve love and care.

Finally, it is important to remember that recovery from narcissistic abuse is a journey, and that it may take time to heal and move on from the trauma. It is okay to take things one step at a time and to be patient with yourself as you work towards healing and recovery. With the right help and support, it is possible to break free from the cycle of abuse and to build a brighter and healthier future.

It is important for victims of narcissistic abuse to understand that they are not alone, and that there are resources and support available to help them heal and recover from the trauma. Some additional resources that may be helpful for victims of narcissistic abuse include:

– Domestic violence hotlines: Many domestic violence hotlines offer support, resources, and counseling for individuals who have experienced abuse. These hotlines can be a safe and confidential way to get help and to find out about additional resources in your area.

– Support groups: Joining a support group can be a helpful way to connect with other individuals who have experienced narcissistic abuse. Support groups can provide a sense of community, as well as a place to share experiences and receive support and guidance.

– Therapy: Working with a therapist or other mental health professional can be a powerful tool in your recovery from narcissistic abuse. A therapist can help you process your experiences, work through your emotions, and develop coping strategies to deal with the aftermath of the abuse.

– Online resources: There are many online resources available for individuals who have experienced narcissistic abuse. These resources can provide information, support, and guidance for those who are seeking to heal and recover from the trauma.

By seeking out these resources and seeking help and support, individuals can take important steps towards healing and recovery from narcissistic abuse. With time and patience, it is possible to break free from the cycle of abuse and to build a brighter and healthier future.

It is important for victims of narcissistic abuse to understand that recovery is a process, and that it may take time to heal and move on from the trauma. It is normal to experience setbacks and challenges along the way, and it is important to be patient with oneself and to allow oneself the time and space to process and heal.

It can be helpful for victims of narcissistic abuse to develop a self-care routine that includes activities that nourish and support their physical, emotional, and mental well-being. This may involve getting enough sleep, eating a healthy diet, exercising, and engaging in activities that bring joy and relaxation.

It is also important for victims to set boundaries and to communicate their needs and limits to others. This may involve cutting off contact or limiting communication with the narcissistic individual or setting limits with other people in your life.

Another important aspect of recovery is building a support system of trusted friends, family members, or a therapist. It can be helpful to have people who can provide love, encouragement, and a listening ear as you work through the recovery process.

Finally, it is important to remember that recovery is a journey, and that it may take time to heal and move on from the trauma. It is okay to take things one step at a time and to be patient with yourself as you work towards healing and recovery. With the right help and support, it is possible to break free from the cycle of abuse and to build a brighter and healthier future.

08: Healing from Narcissistic Abuse

Healing from narcissistic abuse can be a difficult and complex process. Narcissistic abuse is a form of emotional abuse that is inflicted upon a person by a narcissistic individual, who is characterized by an inflated sense of self-importance and a lack of empathy.

The first step in healing from narcissistic abuse is to acknowledge that you have been a victim of abuse. This can be difficult to do, as narcissistic individuals are often skilled at manipulating and controlling their victims, leading them to doubt their own perceptions and experiences. It is important to remember that abuse is never the victim's fault, and that it is not uncommon for victims to have been subjected to gaslighting, which is a form of manipulation that causes the victim to doubt their own memories and perceptions.

Once you have acknowledged that you have been a victim of narcissistic abuse, it is important to seek support from friends, family, or a professional therapist. It can be helpful to speak with someone who can provide an outside perspective and validate your experiences.

It is also important to set boundaries and establish firm limits with the narcissistic individual in your life. This can be challenging, as narcissistic individuals often do not respect boundaries and may attempt to manipulate or control you in order to get their way. However, setting boundaries is crucial in protecting yourself from further abuse and in reclaiming your power.

It is also essential to practice self-care and prioritize your own well-being. This can involve activities such as exercising, getting enough rest, eating a healthy diet, and engaging in activities that bring you joy and relaxation. It is also important to find ways to manage your stress and cope with the trauma of the abuse. This may involve seeking out support from a therapist or counselor, joining a support group, or finding healthy ways to cope with your emotions such as through journaling or practicing mindfulness.

Another important aspect of healing from narcissistic abuse is learning to love and accept yourself. Narcissistic abuse can erode a victim's sense of self-worth and leave them feeling unworthy of love and affection. It is important to remind yourself that you are deserving of love and respect, and to work on building self-confidence and self-esteem.

This can involve engaging in activities that allow you to express yourself creatively, setting and achieving personal goals, and learning to appreciate your own unique qualities and strengths.

It can also be helpful to educate yourself about narcissistic abuse and the tactics that narcissistic individuals use to manipulate and control their victims. This can help you to recognize and defend against these tactics, and to understand the motivations behind the abuse.

Ultimately, healing from narcissistic abuse is a journey that requires patience, self-compassion, and a strong support network. It is important to take things one day at a time and to be gentle with yourself as you work through the healing process. With time, support, and self-care, it is possible to overcome the effects of narcissistic abuse and to rebuild a sense of self-worth and empowerment.

It is also important to work on rebuilding healthy relationships with others. Narcissistic abuse can leave victims feeling isolated and disconnected from others, and it is common for victims to have difficulty trusting others after experiencing abuse. It is important to seek out supportive and healthy relationships, and to work on rebuilding trust with others. This may involve seeking out therapy or joining a support group to work on these issues.

It is also important to work on developing healthy communication skills and learning how to assert your needs and boundaries. This may involve setting limits with others, saying no when appropriate, and learning how to effectively communicate your thoughts and feelings. It can also be helpful to learn how to set and respect boundaries with others, and to recognize when a boundary has been crossed.

Another important aspect of healing from narcissistic abuse is learning to forgive both yourself and the narcissistic individual. Forgiveness does not mean condoning the abuse or absolving the abuser of responsibility, but rather it involves releasing feelings of anger, resentment, and bitterness. Forgiveness can be a difficult process, and it may involve seeking support from a therapist or counselor.

It is also important to remember that healing is a journey and not a destination. It is normal to have ups and downs and to experience setbacks along the way. It is important to be patient with yourself and to recognize that healing takes time.

In conclusion, healing from narcissistic abuse is a complex and difficult process that requires patience, self-compassion, and support. It involves acknowledging the abuse, seeking support, setting boundaries, practicing self-care, rebuilding self-worth, and learning to forgive. With time, support, and self-care, it is possible to overcome the effects of narcissistic abuse and to rebuild a sense of self-worth and empowerment.

It is also important to recognize that healing from narcissistic abuse can be a long-term process, and it may take time to fully understand the impact that the abuse has had on your life. It is important to be patient with yourself and to recognize that it is normal to have good days and bad days as you work through the healing process.

It can be helpful to engage in activities that promote healing and self-care, such as exercising, practicing mindfulness, or engaging in hobbies or activities that bring you joy and relaxation. It is also important to surround yourself with supportive and understanding people who can provide a listening ear and offer encouragement and validation.

It can be helpful to seek out therapy or counseling to work through the emotional and psychological effects of the abuse. A therapist or counselor can provide a safe and supportive space to process your thoughts and feelings and to work on building healthy coping mechanisms.

It is also important to remember that healing from narcissistic abuse is not about returning to the relationship with the narcissistic individual. Instead, it is about moving forward and rebuilding your life in a healthy and empowering way. This may involve finding ways to disconnect from the narcissist, whether through setting boundaries or severing contact altogether.

In summary, healing from narcissistic abuse is a complex and long-term process that requires patience, self-compassion, and support. It involves acknowledging the abuse, seeking support, setting boundaries, practicing self-care, rebuilding self-worth, and learning to forgive. With time, support, and self-care, it is possible to overcome the effects of narcissistic abuse and to rebuild your life in a healthy and empowering way.

It is also important to recognize that healing from narcissistic abuse is not a linear process and that there may be set-backs along the way. It is common to experience a range of emotions as you work through the healing process, and it is important to allow yourself to feel and process these emotions in a healthy way.

It can be helpful to develop healthy coping mechanisms to manage the stress and emotions that may arise as you work through the healing process. This may involve practicing mindfulness, finding healthy outlets for stress such as exercise or creative expression, or seeking support from a therapist or counselor.

It is also important to practice self-compassion and to be kind to yourself as you navigate the healing process. This may involve setting aside time for self-care, such as taking a warm bath or going for a walk, or engaging in activities that bring you joy and relaxation.

It is also important to remember that healing from narcissistic abuse is not about forgetting the abuse or minimizing its impact. It is about acknowledging the abuse, processing the emotions that it has caused, and finding healthy ways to cope with and move beyond the abuse.

In conclusion, healing from narcissistic abuse is a complex and long-term process that requires patience, self-compassion, and support. It involves acknowledging the abuse, seeking support, setting boundaries, practicing self-care, rebuilding self-worth, and learning to forgive. With time, support, and self-care, it is possible to overcome the effects of narcissistic abuse and to rebuild your life in a healthy and empowering way. Remember to be patient with yourself, to practice self-compassion, and to seek out support as you work through the healing process.

09: Coping Strategies for Surviving Narcissistic Abuse

Surviving narcissistic abuse can be a challenging and overwhelming experience, and it is important to have coping strategies in place to help you get through it. Narcissistic abuse is a form of emotional abuse that is inflicted upon a person by a narcissistic individual, who is characterized by an inflated sense of self-importance and a lack of empathy.

One important coping strategy for surviving narcissistic abuse is to establish and maintain strong boundaries. Boundaries are limits that you set with others to protect yourself and to establish what is and is not acceptable behavior. It is important to set boundaries with the narcissistic individual in your life, as they may attempt to manipulate or control you in order to get their way. Setting boundaries can be challenging, as narcissistic individuals often do not respect boundaries, but it is crucial in protecting yourself from further abuse and in reclaiming your power.

Another coping strategy is to seek out a support network of trusted friends, family, or a professional therapist. It can be helpful to speak with someone who can provide an outside perspective and validate your experiences. It is also important to find healthy outlets for your emotions, such as through journaling, talking to a trusted friend or family member, or seeking support from a therapist or counselor.

It is also important to practice self-care and prioritize your own well-being. This can involve activities such as exercising, getting enough rest, eating a healthy diet, and engaging in activities that bring you joy and relaxation. It is also important to find ways to manage your stress and cope with the trauma of the abuse. This may involve seeking out support from a therapist or counselor, joining a support group, or finding healthy ways to cope with your emotions such as through mindfulness or other stress-reduction techniques.

It is also essential to educate yourself about narcissistic abuse and the tactics that narcissistic individuals use to manipulate and control their victims. This can help you to recognize and defend against these tactics, and to understand the motivations behind the abuse. This can be especially helpful in situations where you may still be in contact with the narcissistic individual, as it can give you the knowledge and tools you need to protect yourself from further abuse.

Another coping strategy is to find ways to disconnect from

the narcissistic individual and to create a sense of distance between yourself and the abuse. This may involve setting limits with the narcissistic individual, such as limiting contact or establishing boundaries, or it may involve severing contact altogether. It is important to remember that you have the right to make decisions about your own well-being and to create space for yourself if that is what you need.

It is also important to work on rebuilding your self-worth and self-esteem, as narcissistic abuse can erode these qualities. This may involve engaging in activities that allow you to express yourself creatively, setting and achieving personal goals, and learning to appreciate your own unique qualities and strengths. It can also be helpful to seek out therapy or counseling to work on building self-worth and self-esteem.

Ultimately, coping with narcissistic abuse is a journey that requires patience, self-compassion, and a strong support network. It is important to take things one day at a time and to be gentle with yourself as you work through the healing process. With time, support, and self-care, it is possible to survive narcissistic abuse and to rebuild a sense of self-worth and empowerment.

Another coping strategy is to find healthy ways to cope with the emotions that may arise as a result of the abuse. It is common for victims of narcissistic abuse to experience a range of emotions, including anger, sadness, fear, and guilt. It is important to allow yourself to feel and process these emotions in a healthy way, rather than bottling them up or trying to suppress them.

One way to cope with these emotions is through self-expression, such as through journaling, art, or music. It can also be helpful to engage in activities that allow you to express your emotions in a healthy way, such as through exercise or creative pursuits.

It is also important to seek out healthy outlets for your emotions, such as through talking to a trusted friend or family member, seeking support from a therapist or counselor, or joining a support group. These outlets can provide a safe space to process your thoughts and feelings and can help you to feel less alone as you navigate the challenges of surviving narcissistic abuse.

Another coping strategy is to focus on the present moment and to take things one day at a time. It can be overwhelming to think about the long-term impacts of the abuse, and it is important to focus on what you can control in the present moment. This may involve setting small, achievable goals for yourself, such as going for a walk or spending time with a supportive friend.

It is also important to practice self-compassion and to be kind to yourself as you navigate the challenges of surviving narcissistic abuse. This may involve setting aside time for self-care, such as taking a warm bath or going for a walk, or engaging in activities that bring you joy and relaxation. It is also important to remember that it is okay to have bad days and to give yourself permission to feel and process your emotions.

In conclusion, coping with narcissistic abuse is a challenging and complex process that requires patience, self-compassion, and support. It involves establishing and maintaining boundaries, seeking support, practicing self-care, finding healthy outlets for emotions, educating yourself about narcissistic abuse, and focusing on the present moment.

With time, support, and self-care, it is possible to survive narcissistic abuse and to rebuild a sense of self-worth and empowerment. Remember to be patient with yourself, to practice self-compassion, and to seek out support as you navigate the challenges of surviving narcissistic abuse.

Another coping strategy is to find healthy ways to cope with the aftermath of the abuse, including the trauma and the feelings of grief and loss that may arise. It is common for victims of narcissistic abuse to experience feelings of grief and loss, as they may have lost a sense of self, a sense of trust, or important relationships as a result of the abuse.

One way to cope with these feelings is through therapy or counseling, which can provide a safe and supportive space to process your thoughts and feelings and to work through the grief and loss. It can also be helpful to join a support group, where you can connect with others who have experienced similar challenges and who can provide a sense of community and support.

Another coping strategy is to find healthy outlets for your emotions, such as through talking to a trusted friend or family member, writing in a journal, or engaging in activities that bring you joy and relaxation. It is also important to practice self-care and to prioritize your own well-being, as this can help you to manage the stress and emotions that may arise as you work through the aftermath of the abuse.

It is also important to practice forgiveness, both for yourself and for the narcissistic individual. Forgiveness does not mean condoning the abuse or absolving the abuser of responsibility, but rather it involves releasing feelings of anger, resentment, and bitterness. Forgiveness can be a difficult process, and it may involve seeking support from a therapist or counselor.

It is also important to remember that healing from narcissistic abuse is a journey and not a destination. It is normal to have ups and downs and to experience setbacks along the way. It is important to be patient with yourself and to recognize that healing takes time.

In conclusion, coping with the aftermath of narcissistic abuse is a complex and challenging process that requires patience, self-compassion, and support. It involves finding healthy outlets for emotions, seeking therapy or counseling, practicing self-care, practicing forgiveness, and being patient with yourself. With time, support, and self-care, it is possible to work through the aftermath of narcissistic abuse and to rebuild a sense of self-worth and empowerment. Remember to be patient with yourself, to practice self-compassion, and to seek out support as you work through the challenges of surviving narcissistic abuse.

10: The Role of Therapy in Healing from Narcissistic Abuse

The role of therapy in healing from narcissistic abuse is significant and can be instrumental in helping individuals to work through the emotional and psychological effects of the abuse. Narcissistic abuse is a form of emotional abuse that is inflicted upon a person by a narcissistic individual, who is characterized by an inflated sense of self-importance and a lack of empathy.

One important role of therapy is to provide a safe and supportive space for individuals to process their thoughts and feelings about the abuse. Therapy can provide a place to express and explore the emotions that may arise as a result of the abuse, including anger, sadness, fear, and guilt. It can also provide a space to work through the trauma of the abuse and to develop healthy coping mechanisms.

Another role of therapy is to help individuals to develop healthy coping skills and to build resilience in the face of the challenges that may arise as a result of the abuse. This may involve teaching individuals how to manage their stress and emotions, how to set and maintain boundaries, and how to practice self-care.

Therapy can also play a role in helping individuals to rebuild their self-worth and self-esteem, which may have been eroded as a result of the abuse. This may involve working on building self-confidence and self-acceptance, and learning to appreciate and value one's own unique qualities and strengths.

In addition, therapy can be helpful in helping individuals to develop healthy communication skills and to assert their needs and boundaries. This may involve learning how to effectively express thoughts and feelings, how to set limits with others, and how to recognize when a boundary has been crossed.

Another role of therapy is to help individuals to work through the process of forgiveness, both for themselves and for the narcissistic individual. Forgiveness does not mean condoning the abuse or absolving the abuser of responsibility, but rather it involves releasing feelings of anger, resentment, and bitterness. Forgiveness can be a difficult process, and therapy can provide a safe and supportive space to work through these emotions.

Finally, therapy can help individuals to develop a sense of

empowerment and to rebuild their lives in a healthy and positive way. This may involve working on goals and aspirations, finding ways to disconnect from the narcissistic individual, and building healthy relationships with others.

In conclusion, therapy plays a crucial role in healing from narcissistic abuse. It provides a safe and supportive space to process thoughts and feelings, to develop healthy coping skills and resilience, to rebuild self-worth and self-esteem, to develop healthy communication skills and assertiveness, to work through the process of forgiveness, and to rebuild one's life in a healthy and empowering way. If you are a victim of narcissistic abuse, consider seeking out the support of a qualified therapist or counselor to help you on your journey towards healing and recovery.

Another role of therapy in healing from narcissistic abuse is to help individuals to recognize the patterns of abuse and to understand the tactics that narcissistic individuals use to manipulate and control their victims. This can be especially important in situations where the individual may still be in contact with the narcissistic individual, as it can help them to recognize and defend against these tactics, and to understand the motivations behind the abuse.

Therapy can also be helpful in helping individuals to heal from the trauma of the abuse, which may involve working through the grief and loss that may arise as a result of the abuse. This may involve exploring the impact of the abuse on the individual's sense of self, their relationships, and their sense of trust.

Another role of therapy is to help individuals to develop healthy relationship skills and to rebuild healthy relationships with others. Narcissistic abuse can leave victims feeling isolated and disconnected from others, and it is common for victims to have difficulty trusting others after experiencing abuse. Therapy can provide a safe space to work on rebuilding trust and to learn how to establish and maintain healthy relationships.

It is also important to recognize that healing from narcissistic abuse is a journey and not a destination. It is normal to have ups and downs and to experience setbacks along the way. Therapy can help individuals to be patient with themselves and to recognize that healing takes time.

10: THE ROLE OF THERAPY IN HEALING FROM NAR-CISSISTIC ABUSE

In conclusion, therapy plays a crucial role in healing from narcissistic abuse. It provides a safe and supportive space to process thoughts and feelings, to develop healthy coping skills and resilience, to rebuild self-worth and self-esteem, to develop healthy communication skills and assertiveness, to work through the process of forgiveness, and to rebuild one's life in a healthy and empowering way. It can also help individuals to recognize patterns of abuse, to heal from the trauma of the abuse, and to rebuild healthy relationships with others. If you are a victim of narcissistic abuse, consider seeking out the support of a qualified therapist or counselor to help you on your journey towards healing and recovery.

Narcissistic abuse can be a deeply traumatic and devastating experience for those who have gone through it. It can leave individuals feeling confused, hurt, and unsure of how to move forward with their lives. Therapy can be an essential part of the healing process for those who have experienced narcissistic abuse, as it provides a safe and supportive environment in which to process and make sense of the abuse.

10: THE ROLE OF THERAPY IN HEALING FROM NARCISSISTIC ABUSE

The first step in healing from narcissistic abuse is often acknowledging that the abuse has occurred and that it was not the victim's fault. It can be difficult for individuals who have experienced narcissistic abuse to confront the reality of the abuse, as they may have been made to feel as though they were at fault or that they were responsible for the abuser's behavior. However, it is important to recognize that the abuser is solely responsible for their own actions and that the victim is not to blame for the abuse.

Once an individual has acknowledged the abuse and accepted that it was not their fault, the next step is often to work on rebuilding a sense of self-worth and self-esteem. Narcissistic abusers often seek to undermine their victims' confidence and self-worth, leaving them feeling unsure of themselves and their own value. Therapy can be helpful in this process, as it allows individuals to explore their own thoughts and feelings and to work on rebuilding a positive sense of self.

It is also common for individuals who have experienced narcissistic abuse to struggle with feelings of anxiety, depression, and post-traumatic stress disorder (PTSD). Therapy can be an important tool in addressing and managing these feelings, helping individuals to develop coping mechanisms and to learn how to regulate their emotions.

In addition to individual therapy, group therapy can also be beneficial for those who have experienced narcissistic abuse. Group therapy provides a sense of community and support, allowing individuals to connect with others who have experienced similar situations and to share their experiences and insights. Group therapy can also be helpful in normalizing the feelings and experiences of those who have been through narcissistic abuse, as it allows individuals to see that they are not alone and that others have been through similar experiences.

It is important for individuals who are seeking therapy for narcissistic abuse to find a therapist who is experienced in working with this type of abuse. A therapist who is knowledgeable about narcissistic abuse can provide valuable support and guidance as individuals work through the healing process. It is also important for individuals to feel comfortable and safe with their therapist, as this will facilitate a more productive and beneficial therapeutic relationship.

10: THE ROLE OF THERAPY IN HEALING FROM NARCISSISTIC ABUSE

In conclusion, therapy can play a crucial role in healing from narcissistic abuse. By providing a safe and supportive environment in which to process the abuse and rebuild a sense of self-worth, therapy can help individuals to move forward with their lives and to reclaim their sense of agency and autonomy. If you or someone you know has experienced narcissistic abuse, seeking out therapy can be an important step in the healing process.

11: The Importance of Self-Care after Narcissistic Abuse

Self-care is an essential part of the healing process after experiencing narcissistic abuse. Narcissistic abuse can be a deeply traumatic and devastating experience, leaving individuals feeling drained, exhausted, and unsure of how to move forward. It is important for individuals to prioritize their own well-being and to take care of themselves in order to facilitate healing and recovery.

One of the first steps in the self-care process is to prioritize self-compassion. It is common for individuals who have experienced narcissistic abuse to blame themselves for the abuse, feeling as though they could have done something to prevent it. It is important to remember that the abuse was not the victim's fault and that they are not to blame for the abuser's behavior. Practicing self-compassion can help individuals to let go of self-blame and to be kind and understanding towards themselves as they heal.

Another important aspect of self-care is taking time for oneself. After experiencing narcissistic abuse, it is common for individuals to feel overwhelmed and burnt out. It is important to take time for oneself and to prioritize one's own needs and desires. This can include activities such as getting enough rest, engaging in hobbies and activities that bring joy, and setting boundaries with others.

It is also important to practice good self-care habits, such as maintaining a healthy diet, getting regular exercise, and engaging in relaxation techniques such as meditation or yoga. These habits can help to reduce stress and promote overall well-being.

In addition to physical self-care, it is also important to prioritize emotional and mental well-being. This can include seeking out therapy to process the abuse and to work through any lingering emotions or trauma. It can also be helpful to practice mindfulness and to engage in activities that promote emotional well-being, such as journaling or talking to a trusted friend or family member.

It is important to remember that self-care looks different for everyone and that what works for one person may not work for another. It is important to experiment and find what works best for oneself in terms of self-care.

It is also important to recognize that self-care is not selfish.

11: THE IMPORTANCE OF SELF-CARE AFTER NARCISS-ISTIC ABUSE

Taking care of oneself is necessary in order to be able to effectively care for others and to fully engage in one's life. It is not a luxury, but rather a necessity for healing and recovery.

In conclusion, self-care is an essential part of the healing process after experiencing narcissistic abuse. By prioritizing self-compassion, taking time for oneself, and practicing good self-care habits, individuals can facilitate their own healing and recovery and work towards rebuilding their lives.

It can be challenging to prioritize self-care after experiencing narcissistic abuse, especially if the abuser was controlling or manipulative. It may be necessary to set boundaries with the abuser and to limit or cut off contact in order to prioritize one's own well-being. This can be difficult, especially if there are shared children or financial ties, but it is important to prioritize one's own safety and well-being.

It can also be helpful to seek out a support system of trusted friends and family members who can provide emotional support and practical assistance as needed. It is important to surround oneself with people who are supportive and understanding and who can provide a sense of community as one navigates the healing process.

It is also important to recognize that healing from narcissistic abuse is a journey and that it may not happen overnight. It is normal to have ups and downs and to experience a range of emotions as one processes the abuse and works towards healing. It is important to be patient with oneself and to allow oneself the time and space to heal at one's own pace.

In conclusion, the importance of self-care after experiencing narcissistic abuse cannot be overstated. By prioritizing self-compassion, taking time for oneself, and seeking out a supportive network of friends and family, individuals can begin to rebuild their lives and to move forward in a positive and healthy way. It is a journey, but with patience and self-care, healing is possible.

It is also important to recognize that healing from narcissistic abuse is not a linear process and that there may be setbacks along the way. It is common for individuals to experience triggers that can bring up memories of the abuse and to feel overwhelmed by emotions. It is important to have coping mechanisms in place to deal with these triggers and to take care of oneself during these times.

It may be necessary to seek additional support during times of increased stress or difficulty. This can include seeking out therapy or support groups, or even taking a break from certain activities or responsibilities to focus on self-care. It is important to prioritize one's own well-being and to do what is necessary to take care of oneself during these times.

It is also important to remember that healing from narcissistic abuse is not about forgetting the past or pretending that the abuse never happened. It is about acknowledging the abuse and the impact it had, and then finding ways to move forward and to create a healthy and fulfilling life. This may involve setting boundaries, learning to advocate for oneself, and finding ways to cope with the lasting effects of the abuse.

It is also important to recognize that healing is not a solo journey and that it is okay to ask for help. It can be difficult to navigate the healing process on one's own, and seeking out support and guidance from trusted friends, family, or a therapist can be an important part of the process.

11: THE IMPORTANCE OF SELF-CARE AFTER NARCISS-ISTIC ABUSE

In conclusion, healing from narcissistic abuse is a complex and nuanced process that requires patience, self-compassion, and a willingness to prioritize one's own well-being. It is a journey that involves acknowledging the past and the impact of the abuse, while also finding ways to move forward and create a healthy and fulfilling life. By seeking out support and practicing self-care, individuals can work towards healing and towards creating a life that is meaningful and fulfilling.

Another aspect of healing from narcissistic abuse is learning to recognize and avoid toxic or abusive relationships in the future. This may involve learning to set boundaries, assert oneself, and advocate for one's own needs and desires. It can also involve learning to recognize the warning signs of narcissistic abuse, such as a lack of empathy, a tendency towards manipulation or control, and a focus on one's own needs at the expense of others.

It can be helpful to work with a therapist or coach who is experienced in working with individuals who have experienced narcissistic abuse, as they can provide guidance and support as one navigates the process of recognizing and avoiding toxic relationships. It may also be helpful to seek out resources and support groups that can provide additional guidance and support.

In addition to seeking out support and learning to recognize and avoid toxic relationships, it is also important to focus on self-growth and personal development. This can involve finding activities and hobbies that bring joy and meaning, setting goals and working towards achieving them, and finding ways to express oneself and one's unique talents and interests.

Self-growth and personal development can be an important part of the healing process, as it allows individuals to move beyond the trauma of the abuse and to create a life that is fulfilling and meaningful. It can also help to rebuild a sense of self-worth and confidence, which may have been damaged as a result of the abuse.

In conclusion, healing from narcissistic abuse involves a range of activities and strategies, including seeking out support, practicing self-care, learning to recognize and avoid toxic relationships, and focusing on self-growth and personal development. By engaging in these activities, individuals can work towards rebuilding their lives and towards creating a future that is healthy, fulfilling, and free from abuse.

12: Breaking the Cycle: How to Avoid Narcissistic Relationships

Narcissistic relationships can be deeply damaging and traumatic, leaving individuals feeling hurt, confused, and unsure of how to move forward. It is important for individuals who have experienced narcissistic abuse to take steps to break the cycle and to avoid future narcissistic relationships.

One of the first steps in breaking the cycle is to educate oneself about narcissistic personality disorder and the signs of narcissistic abuse. It is important to recognize the patterns of behavior that are typical of narcissistic individuals and to be aware of the warning signs of narcissistic abuse. Some common signs of narcissistic abuse include a lack of empathy, a tendency towards manipulation or control, and a focus on one's own needs at the expense of others.

It is also important to recognize the ways in which narcissistic individuals may try to manipulate or control their victims. Narcissistic individuals may try to gaslight their victims, making them doubt their own perceptions and memories. They may also try to isolate their victims from friends and family, making them feel dependent on the abuser. By being aware of these tactics, individuals can better protect themselves from falling victim to narcissistic abuse.

In addition to educating oneself about narcissistic personality disorder and the signs of narcissistic abuse, it is also important to set boundaries and to assert oneself in relationships. This may involve setting limits on what one is willing to tolerate in a relationship and standing up for oneself when those boundaries are violated. It may also involve learning to advocate for one's own needs and desires and to communicate openly and honestly with others.

It can be helpful to seek out support and guidance from trusted friends and family members, as well as from therapists or coaches who are experienced in working with individuals who have experienced narcissistic abuse. These individuals can provide valuable perspective and guidance as one navigates the process of breaking the cycle and avoiding future narcissistic relationships.

It is also important to prioritize self-care and to focus on one's own well-being. This may involve setting aside time for oneself, engaging in activities that bring joy and meaning, and practicing good self-care habits such as maintaining a healthy diet and getting regular exercise. Taking care of oneself can help to build confidence and self-worth, which can be important in avoiding future narcissistic relationships.

In conclusion, breaking the cycle of narcissistic relationships involves educating oneself about narcissistic personality disorder and the signs of narcissistic abuse, setting boundaries and asserting oneself, seeking out support, and prioritizing self-care. By engaging in these activities, individuals can better protect themselves from falling victim to narcissistic abuse and can work towards creating healthy, fulfilling relationships in the future.

It is also important to recognize that breaking the cycle of narcissistic relationships is a process and that it may not happen overnight. It may take time to unlearn patterns of behavior that have been reinforced by past narcissistic relationships and to develop new, healthier ways of relating to others. It is important to be patient with oneself and to allow oneself the time and space to work through this process.

It may also be helpful to work on building self-esteem and self-worth. Narcissistic individuals often seek out individuals with low self-esteem, as they are more likely to be swayed by the abuser's manipulations. By building a strong sense of self-worth and self-esteem, individuals can become more resilient to the manipulations of narcissistic individuals.

It is also important to recognize that it is not uncommon for individuals who have experienced narcissistic abuse to attract narcissistic individuals in the future. This may be due to a pattern of seeking out individuals who will reinforce negative beliefs about oneself, or it may be a result of a lack of awareness of the warning signs of narcissistic abuse. It is important to be aware of this pattern and to actively work to break it by educating oneself about narcissistic personality disorder and the signs of narcissistic abuse, setting boundaries, and seeking out supportive and healthy relationships.

In conclusion, breaking the cycle of narcissistic relationships involves a range of activities and strategies, including educating oneself about narcissistic personality disorder, setting boundaries and asserting oneself, seeking out support, prioritizing self-care, and working on building self-esteem and self-worth. By engaging in these activities, individuals can better protect themselves from falling victim to narcissistic abuse and can work towards creating healthy, fulfilling relationships in the future. It is a process, but with patience and persistence, it is possible to break the cycle and to create a life that is free from narcissistic abuse.

It is also important to recognize that breaking the cycle of narcissistic relationships is not just about avoiding narcissistic individuals, but also about healing from the trauma of the abuse. This may involve seeking out therapy to process the abuse and to work through any lingering emotions or trauma. It may also involve finding ways to cope with the lasting effects of the abuse, such as anxiety, depression, or post-traumatic stress disorder (PTSD).

It is important to recognize that healing from narcissistic abuse is a journey and that it may take time. It is normal to have ups and downs and to experience a range of emotions as one processes the abuse and works towards healing. It is important to be patient with oneself and to allow oneself the time and space to heal at one's own pace.

In addition to seeking out therapy, it can be helpful to find other sources of support, such as support groups or trusted friends and family members. It is important to surround oneself with individuals who are supportive and understanding and who can provide a sense of community as one navigates the healing process.

It is also important to recognize that breaking the cycle of narcissistic relationships is not about forgetting the past or pretending that the abuse never happened. It is about acknowledging the abuse and the impact it had, and then finding ways to move forward and to create a healthy and fulfilling life. This may involve setting boundaries, learning to advocate for oneself, and finding ways to cope with the lasting effects of the abuse.

In conclusion, breaking the cycle of narcissistic relationships involves not just avoiding narcissistic individuals, but also healing from the trauma of the abuse. This may involve seeking out therapy, finding support, and focusing on self-care and self-growth. By engaging in these activities, individuals can work towards healing and towards creating a future that is healthy, fulfilling, and free from abuse.

It may also be helpful to work on building healthy communication skills as a way to break the cycle of narcissistic relationships. Narcissistic individuals often use communication as a way to manipulate and control their victims, and learning healthy communication skills can help individuals to protect themselves from falling victim to this type of abuse.

Healthy communication skills include the ability to express oneself clearly and assertively, to listen actively and empathetically, and to resolve conflicts in a healthy way. It may be helpful to seek out resources or training on healthy communication skills or to work with a therapist or coach who can provide guidance and support in this area.

Another important aspect of breaking the cycle of narcissistic relationships is learning to recognize and trust one's own instincts and boundaries. It is common for individuals who have experienced narcissistic abuse to doubt their own perceptions and to feel unsure of what they want and need. It is important to tune in to one's own feelings and to listen to one's own needs and desires. Setting boundaries and advocating for oneself can be an important part of this process.

It is also important to recognize that breaking the cycle of narcissistic relationships does not mean that all relationships will be perfect or free from conflict. Healthy relationships involve give and take and require effort and communication from both parties. However, by learning to recognize and trust one's own instincts and boundaries and by building healthy communication skills, individuals can work towards creating relationships that are healthy, fulfilling, and free from abuse.

In conclusion, breaking the cycle of narcissistic relationships involves a range of activities and strategies, including seeking out therapy, finding support, practicing self-care and self-growth, building healthy communication skills, and learning to recognize and trust one's own instincts and boundaries. By engaging in these activities, individuals can work towards healing from the trauma of narcissistic abuse and towards creating a future that is healthy, fulfilling, and free from abuse.

13: Moving Forward: Building a Healthy Life after Narcissistic Abuse

Moving forward and building a healthy life after experiencing narcissistic abuse can be a challenging but rewarding process. It involves acknowledging the abuse and the impact it had, while also finding ways to move beyond the trauma and to create a fulfilling and meaningful life.

One of the first steps in this process is to prioritize self-care and to take care of one's own well-being. This may involve setting aside time for oneself, engaging in activities that bring joy and meaning, and practicing good self-care habits such as maintaining a healthy diet and getting regular exercise. It is important to remember that self-care is not selfish, but rather a necessary part of the healing process and of building a healthy life.

Another important aspect of moving forward is seeking out support and guidance from trusted friends and family members, as well as from therapists or coaches who are experienced in working with individuals who have experienced narcissistic abuse. These individuals can provide valuable perspective and guidance as one navigates the process of healing and building a healthy life.

It is also important to work on building healthy communication skills and to learn how to effectively advocate for oneself and one's own needs and desires. This may involve setting boundaries and learning to assert oneself in relationships. It may also involve learning to recognize and avoid toxic or abusive relationships in the future.

In addition to these strategies, it can be helpful to focus on self-growth and personal development. This may involve finding activities and hobbies that bring joy and meaning, setting goals and working towards achieving them, and finding ways to express oneself and one's unique talents and interests. Self-growth and personal development can be an important part of the healing process, as it allows individuals to move beyond the trauma of the abuse and to create a life that is fulfilling and meaningful.

It is also important to recognize that moving forward and building a healthy life after narcissistic abuse is a journey and that it may not happen overnight. It is normal to have ups and downs and to experience a range of emotions as one processes the abuse and works towards healing. It is important to be patient with oneself and to allow oneself the time and space to heal at one's own pace.

In conclusion, moving forward and building a healthy life after narcissistic abuse involves a range of activities and strategies, including prioritizing self-care, seeking out support, building healthy communication skills, focusing on self-growth and personal development, and being patient with oneself. By engaging in these activities, individuals can work towards healing from the trauma of narcissistic abuse and towards creating a future that is healthy, fulfilling, and free from abuse.

It can also be helpful to find ways to cope with the lasting effects of the abuse, such as anxiety, depression, or post-traumatic stress disorder (PTSD). This may involve seeking out therapy or support groups, or finding healthy ways to manage stress, such as through exercise or relaxation techniques.

It is important to recognize that healing from narcissistic abuse is a process and that it may involve revisiting and processing difficult emotions and memories. It is normal to experience a range of emotions as one works through the healing process, and it is important to allow oneself the time and space to process these emotions in a healthy way.

It may also be helpful to find ways to connect with others who have experienced similar types of abuse. Support groups or online communities can provide a sense of community and a sense of connection with others who understand the unique challenges and experiences of narcissistic abuse.

Another important aspect of moving forward and building a healthy life is learning to forgive oneself for any perceived mistakes or for staying in the abusive relationship for longer than one wished. It is important to recognize that narcissistic abuse is often characterized by manipulation and control, and that it is not the victim's fault. It is also important to recognize that healing is a process and that it is normal to have setbacks along the way.

In conclusion, moving forward and building a healthy life after narcissistic abuse involves a range of activities and strategies, including seeking out therapy or support, finding healthy ways to cope with the lasting effects of the abuse, connecting with others who have experienced similar types of abuse, and learning to forgive oneself. By engaging in these activities, individuals can work towards healing from the trauma of narcissistic abuse and towards creating a future that is healthy, fulfilling, and free from abuse.

It can also be helpful to work on rebuilding one's sense of self and one's sense of identity after experiencing narcissistic abuse. Narcissistic individuals often attempt to manipulate and control their victims by undermining their sense of self and their sense of identity. Rebuilding a strong sense of self and a healthy sense of identity can be an important part of the healing process.

This may involve finding activities and hobbies that bring joy and meaning, setting goals and working towards achieving them, and finding ways to express oneself and one's unique talents and interests. It may also involve seeking out therapy or support to work through any lingering issues related to self-esteem or self-worth.

It is also important to recognize that moving forward and building a healthy life after narcissistic abuse is not about forgetting the past or pretending that the abuse never happened. It is about acknowledging the abuse and the impact it had, and then finding ways to move forward and to create a healthy and fulfilling life. This may involve setting boundaries, learning to advocate for oneself, and finding ways to cope with the lasting effects of the abuse.

In conclusion, moving forward and building a healthy life after narcissistic abuse involves a range of activities and strategies, including seeking out therapy or support, finding healthy ways to cope with the lasting effects of the abuse, connecting with others who have experienced similar types of abuse, learning to forgive oneself, and rebuilding a strong sense of self and identity. It is a journey that requires patience, self-compassion, and a willingness to prioritize one's own well-being. By engaging in these activities and strategies, individuals can work towards healing from the trauma of narcissistic abuse and towards creating a future that is healthy, fulfilling, and free from abuse.

It is also important to recognize that moving forward does not mean that all challenges or difficulties will disappear. Life is unpredictable and there will always be ups and downs. However, by focusing on self-care, seeking out support, and building healthy coping skills, individuals can work towards building a strong foundation of resilience that will help them to navigate life's challenges and to create a healthy, fulfilling life.

It is also important to remember that it is okay to ask for help when needed. It is not uncommon for individuals who have experienced narcissistic abuse to feel isolated or un-supported, and seeking out help and support from trusted friends, family, or a therapist can be an important part of the healing process.

In conclusion, moving forward and building a healthy life after narcissistic abuse involves a range of activities and strategies, including prioritizing self-care, seeking out sup-port, building healthy coping skills, rebuilding a strong sense of self and identity, and remembering that it is okay to ask for help when needed. By engaging in these activities, individuals can work towards healing from the trauma of narcissistic abuse and towards creating a future that is healthy, fulfilling, and free from abuse. It is important to re-cognize that this process takes time and requires patience, self-compassion, and a willingness to prioritize one's own well-being.

One final aspect of moving forward and building a healthy life after narcissistic abuse is finding ways to let go of the past and to create a new future. This may involve finding ways to forgive the abuser, either for oneself or as a way to move on from the abuse. It may also involve finding ways to let go of the pain and trauma of the abuse and to focus on building a new, healthy life.

This process may involve finding ways to cope with any lingering feelings of anger, hurt, or resentment. It may also involve finding healthy ways to express and process these emotions, such as through therapy or journaling. It is important to recognize that letting go of the past is a process and that it may take time, but it is an important step in moving forward and building a healthy life after narcissistic abuse.

In conclusion, moving forward and building a healthy life after narcissistic abuse involves a range of activities and strategies, including prioritizing self-care, seeking out support, building healthy coping skills, rebuilding a strong sense of self and identity, remembering that it is okay to ask for help when needed, and finding ways to let go of the past and to create a new future. By engaging in these activities, individuals can work towards healing from the trauma of narcissistic abuse and towards creating a future that is healthy, fulfilling, and free from abuse.

Thank You

As we reach the end of this book, I want to say thanks for reading this book.

I want to get this information out to as many people as possible. If you found this book helpful, I would greatly appreciate you leaving me a review. This helps others find the book as well.

Disclaimer

This document is geared towards providing exact and reliable information in regards to the topic and issue covered. The publication is sold on the idea that the publisher is not required to render an accounting, officially permitted, or otherwise, qualified services. If advice is necessary, legal, financial, medical or professional, a practiced individual in the profession should be ordered.

This information is not presented by a financial or medical practitioner and is for entertainment, educational and informational purposes only. The content is not intended as a substitute for professional medical advice, diagnosis, or treatment. Always seek the advice of your physician or other qualified health care provider with any questions you may have regarding a medical condition. Never disregard professional medical advice or delay in seeking it because of something you have read.

The information provided herein is stated to be truthful and consistent, in that any liability, in terms of inattention or otherwise, by any usage or abuse of any policies, processes, or directions contained within is the solitary and utter responsibility of the recipient reader. Under no circumstances

DISCLAIMER

will any legal responsibility or blame be held against the publisher for any reparation, damages, or monetary loss due to the information herein, either directly or indirectly.

www.ingramcontent.com/pod-product-compliance
Lightning Source LLC
Chambersburg PA
CBHW060519130626
46553CB00002B/566